D0589144

WALTHAM FOREST LIBRARIES

904 000 00257656

# WeightWatchers®

# COOK SMART baking

Great-tasting baking recipes for every occasion,
all updated with *ProPoints*® values

SIMON &
SCHUSTER
ILLUSTRATED

London · New York · Sydney · Toronto

A CBS COMPANY

First published in Great Britain by Simon & Schuster UK Ltd, 2009
This edition published 2011
A CBS Company

Copyright © 2009, Weight Watchers International, Inc.
Simon & Schuster Illustrated Books, Simon & Schuster UK Ltd, First Floor, 222 Gray's Inn Road, London WC1X 8HB

This book is copyright under the Berne Convention.
No reproduction without permission. All rights reserved.

Weight Watchers, *ProPoints* and the *ProPoints* icon are trademarks of Weight Watchers International, Inc. and are used under license by
Simon & Schuster (UK) Ltd.

Weight Watchers Publications Team: Jane Griffiths, Donna Watts and Nina McKerlie.

Recipes written by: Sue Ashworth, Sue Beveridge, Tamsin Burnett-Hall, Cas Clarke, Siân Davies, R
Penny Stephens, Wendy Veale and Weight Watchers Leaders and Members.

Photography by: Iain Bagwell, Steve Baxter and Steve Lee.
Design and typesetting by James Marks and Tiger Media Ltd.

Colour reproduction by Dot Gradations Ltd, UK
Printed and bound in China

A CIP catalogue for this book is available from the British Library

ISBN 978-0-85720-451-6

1 3 5 7 9 10 8 6 4 2

| Waltham Forest Libraries | |
| --- | --- |
| 904 000 00257656 | |
| Askews & Holts | 12-Mar-2013 |
| 641.815 | £14.99 |
| 3821745 | |

Pictured on the front cover: Yorkshire Curd Tarts page 96, Blueberry Cookies page 52, Better Brownies page 34, Nectarine and Strawberry Tart page 92.
Pictured on the back cover: Apple and Apricot Muffins page 68, Fresh Fig Tart page102, Summer Fruit Profiteroles page 144, Lemon and Ginger Roulade page 36.
Pictured on the introduction: Squishy Squash Ginger Cake page 22, Cinnamon Prune Buns page 80, Fresh Fig Tart page 102, Hazelnut Meringue Roulade page 148.

 **ProPoints**® value logo: You'll find this easy to read *ProPoints* value logo on every recipe throughout this book. The logo represents the number of *ProPoints* values per serving each recipe contains. It is not an indication of the fillingness of a recipe.

Weight Watchers *ProPoints* Weight Loss System is a simple way to lose weight. As part of the Weight Watchers *ProPoints* plan you'll enjoy eating delicious, healthy, filling foods that help to keep you feeling satisfied for longer and in control of your portions.

**V** This symbol denotes a vegetarian recipe and assumes that, where relevant, free range eggs, vegetarian cheese, vegetarian virtually fat free fromage frais, vegetarian low fat crème fraîche and vegetarian low fat yogurts are used. Virtually fat free fromage frais, low fat crème fraîche and low fat yogurts may contain traces of gelatine so they are not always vegetarian. Please check the labels.

**✱** This symbol denotes a dish that can be frozen. Unless otherwise stated, freeze the finished dish for up to 3 months. Defrost and heat, if applicable, until piping hot throughout.

### Recipe notes
**Egg size:** Medium, unless otherwise stated.
**Raw eggs:** Only the freshest eggs should be used. Pregnant women, the elderly and children should avoid recipes with eggs that are not fully cooked or raw.
**All fruits and vegetables:** Medium sized, unless otherwise stated.
**Stock:** Stock cubes used in recipes, unless otherwise stated. These should be prepared according to packet instructions.
**Recipe timings:** These are approximate and meant to be guidelines. Please note that the preparation time includes all the steps up to and following the main cooking time(s).
**Microwaves:** Timings and temperatures are for a standard 800 W microwave. If necessary, adjust to your own microwave.
**Low fat spread:** Where a recipe states to use a low fat spread, a light spread with a fat content of no less than 38% should be used.
**Low fat soft cheese:** Where low fat soft cheese is specified in a recipe, this refers to soft cheese with a fat content of 5% or less, such as Philadelphia Extra Light.

# Contents

Introduction 5

Kitchen Basics 6

Cakes and Teabreads 8

Biscuits, Bread and Bakes 48

Pies, Tarts and Pastries 90

Baked Desserts and Puddings 118

Index 158

# Introduction

If you enjoy baking, this is the book for you. Now completely updated with new *ProPoints* values, it's brimming with tempting cakes, biscuits, tarts and baked desserts that your family and friends will love. As well as delicious recipes, you'll find hints and tips throughout the book. Extra information on these pages should also help you make the most of your time when creating these wonderful dishes.

## About Weight Watchers

For more than 40 years Weight Watchers has been helping people around the world to lose weight using a long term sustainable approach. Weight Watchers successful weight loss system is based on four tried and trusted principles:

- Eating healthily
- Being more active
- Adjusting behaviour to help weight loss
- Getting support in weekly meetings

Our unique *ProPoints* system empowers you to manage your food plan and make wise recipe choices for a healthier, happier you.

# Kitchen Basics

## Temperature and timing

Ovens tend to vary in efficiency, but generally speaking conventional and gas ovens need to be preheated for 10–15 minutes, while fan ovens don't need preheating. It is important for the shelves to be correctly placed (high, middle, low) as this can be critical to the success of a recipe.

## Cake, muffin and bun tins

Use good quality non stick tins and, for the best results, try to keep to the size mentioned in the recipe. Either spray the bottom and sides of the tin with a little low fat cooking spray or use baking parchment or a silicone liner to line them, depending on the instructions given.

A muffin tin is usually divided into 12 with a depth of 3 cm (1¼ inches). When baking muffins and small cakes, put the batter into individual paper cases so that they don't break when you take them out. A bun tin is shallow with 12 indentations for individual buns.

## Pastry tins

A metal, loose-bottomed flan tin is great for pies and tarts as the removable base makes it easy to get the pastry out without damaging it. Metal is also a good heat conductor, so the pastry cooks through. Flan tins will not need greasing. Simply put the pastry over the rolling pin and unroll over the tin, easing it into the edges. A good tip is to prick the pastry with a fork to prevent the pastry base from rising during cooking.

## Leaving a cake in the tin

The recipes will give advice on how long to leave the cake in the tin before turning it out. This is to allow the cake to shrink slightly so it comes out easily. It will also be firmer if left for a while.

## Flour

Always sift flour first to get rid of impurities and to help it blend more easily with other dry ingredients, such as raising agents, ground spices or sugar.

- **White plain** – good for scones and other bakes when used with a raising agent. Brown flour has more bran.
- **White self raising** – contains self raising agents for a consistent result.
- **Wholemeal** – can be substituted for white plain flour if you prefer, or used half and half if you want a lighter bake.
- **Strong bread flour** – contains higher percentages of gluten to give bread more elasticity. Strong bread flour can be bought as white, brown or wholemeal.
- **Cornflour** – made from maize, this very soft white flour gives a light texture to cakes and biscuits.
- **Sauce flour** – good to use as a thickening agent without having to add any fat.
- **Polenta** (cornmeal) – an Italian golden cornmeal, ground from dried corn or maize.

## Raising agents

These are additional aids to rising, as the air incorporated during mixing is not enough to make a bread or cake rise.

- **Yeast** – usually used during bread making to make the dough rise. Most people don't have access to fresh yeast, so use dried. It is always a good idea to activate the yeast first in warm liquid rather than put it straight into the flour. It only takes a minute, but the results are better.
- **Bicarbonate of soda** – an alkaline raising agent.
- **Cream of tartar** – an acidic raising agent.
- **Baking powder** – a combination of the two raising agents, baking powder has added dried starch to prevent the reaction of bicarbonate of soda and cream of tartar when stored.

## Sugar

When baking muffins, scones and cakes, the type of sugar will affect the flavour. In bread making, sugar is used mainly to activate the yeast, so the type is not as important.

- **Artificial sweetener** – a low calorie replacement for sugar.
- **Caster** – commonly used in baking as it is fine grained.
- **Granulated** – crunchier than caster sugar.
- **Icing sugar** – a fine powder used to make icing and to sprinkle over cakes or puddings.
- **Soft light and dark brown** – fine, moist brown sugar with molasses.
- **Muscovado** – unrefined, raw cane sugar. Light or dark brown and finely grained varieties are available. Muscovado is good for flapjacks.

## Fats and oils

- **Low fat spread –** always use a low fat spread that has a fat content of at least 38%. All the recipes in the book specify low fat spread.
- **Low fat cooking spray** – works as a substitute for oil. You can use it for greasing, frying, roasting, browning and grilling. You can get low fat cooking spray with a sunflower or olive oil base, depending on your preference.

## Chocolate and cocoa powder

Use good quality chocolate (preferably at least 70% cocoa solids) for cooking so that you get the rich chocolate taste without having to use so much.

A tub of good cocoa powder is a store cupboard basic if you make cakes and muffins. Always sieve cocoa powder for baking, as it can be lumpy.

## Dried fruit

Most dried fruits are ready to eat and don't need soaking, but if the packet is not marked 'ready to eat' you can soak the fruit in a little water first to plump it up. Always wash and dry glacé cherries.

# Cakes and Teabreads

Teatime can always be a special occasion with these home made cake recipes that cater for every taste. There are fruit cakes like Peach Crumble Cake, traybakes such as Carrot and Pineapple Squares, a delicious spicy Lemon and Ginger Roulade and, of course, chocolate recipes like Chocolate Mocha Fudge Cake.

Nothing goes better with a cup of tea or coffee than delicious home made cake

# Pear and Chocolate Cake

If you are in need of a chocolate fix, this will certainly do the job. It has to be one of the easiest cakes you will ever make, and one of the most delicious you've ever tasted.

**Makes 8 slices**

**low fat cooking spray**
**150 g (5½ oz) plain white flour**
**1 teaspoon baking powder**
**50 g (1¾ oz) fructose**
**150 g (5½ oz) low fat spread**
**3 eggs**
**150 g (5½ oz) dark chocolate, chopped roughly**
**1 pear, peeled and diced**

8 **ProPoints** values per serving
64 **ProPoints** values per recipe

295 **calories** per serving

Takes **10 minutes** to prepare + cooling,
**50 minutes** to bake

v

* not recommended

1 Preheat the oven to Gas Mark 4/180°C/fan oven 160°C. Spray a 900 g (2 lb) loaf tin with the cooking spray and line the bottom with greaseproof paper.

2 Place the flour, baking powder, fructose and low fat spread in a food processor and blend for 3–4 seconds to mix them together. Add the eggs and blend for another 6–8 seconds.

3 Stir in the chocolate and the pear and pour the mixture into the prepared tin.

4 Bake for 45–50 minutes until risen and golden and a knife comes out clean (apart from melted chocolate).

5 Place the cake on to a rack until cool, then remove from the tin and serve in slices.

Tip To prevent making a mess when chopping chocolate, try bashing it with a rolling pin while it is still in the foil wrapper – you can feel how small the pieces are before opening it.

# Peach Crumble Cake

Ideal with a cup of coffee, this cake can also be served warm as a pudding with 150 g (5½ oz) low fat custard per person, for an extra 3 *ProPoints* values per serving.

**Serves 12**

**low fat cooking spray**
**275 g (9½ oz) self raising flour**
**1 teaspoon cinnamon**
**salt**
**125 g (4½ oz) low fat spread**
**125 g (4½ oz) soft light brown sugar**
**3 eggs, beaten**
**200 g (7 oz) low fat natural yogurt**
**410 g can peach slices in juice, drained**

**5 *ProPoints*** values per serving
**59 *ProPoints*** values per recipe

**196 calories** per serving

Takes **10 minutes** to prepare + cooling,
**50 minutes** to bake

V

✽ recommended

1 Preheat the oven to Gas Mark 4/180°C/fan oven 160°C. Spray a 20 cm (8 inch) springform cake tin with the cooking spray and line it with baking parchment.

2 Sift the flour, cinnamon and a pinch of salt into a mixing bowl. Rub in the low fat spread until the mixture is crumbly, then stir in the sugar. Weigh out 80 g (3 oz) of the mixture into a small bowl for the topping and set this aside.

3 Mix the eggs and yogurt into the remaining flour mixture to form a smooth batter, then pour into the prepared cake tin.

4 Pat the peaches dry on kitchen paper, then arrange on top of the cake.

5 Scatter with the reserved crumb mixture, then bake the cake in the oven for 45–50 minutes, or until a skewer inserted in the centre comes out clean. Cool on a wire rack. The cake can be stored for 2–3 days.

**Save time** If you're short of time, opt for canned fruit, which saves you the trouble of peeling and de-seeding the fruit yourself. However, if you do, look for fruit canned in natural juice rather than syrup as it's a lower *ProPoints* value option.

# Moist Mango Cake

This exotically flavoured, light but moist cake is a lovely teatime treat. It works well as a dessert served with 1 tablespoon virtually fat free fromage frais, for 1 additional *ProPoints* value per serving.

**Serves 12**

**low fat cooking spray**
**2 egg whites**
**1 egg, separated**
**8 tablespoons artificial sweetener**
**425 g can mango slices in juice, drained and puréed in a food processor**
**2 drops vanilla essence**
**1 tablespoon sunflower oil**
**125 g (4½ oz) self raising flour**
**1 teaspoon icing sugar, for dusting**

2 *ProPoints* values per serving
18 *ProPoints* values per recipe

C  **80 calories** per serving

Takes **20 minutes** to prepare + cooling,
**45 minutes** to bake

V

✳  not recommended

1  Preheat the oven to Gas Mark 4/180°C/fan oven 160°C and spray a 20 cm (8 inch) round spring form baking tin with the cooking spray.

2  In a large bowl, whisk the egg whites until they form stiff peaks. In another large bowl, mix the sweetener, egg yolk, mango purée, vanilla essence, oil and flour.

3  Fold in the whisked egg whites and then pour into the prepared tin. Bake for 45 minutes, until golden and risen and a skewer inserted in the middle comes out clean.

4  Allow to cool before removing from the tin, then dust with icing sugar to serve.

**Cooking basics** How to whisk egg whites: use eggs that have been left at room temperature and a large mixing bowl that is clean and dry. First separate the eggs and put the whites in the bowl, making sure that they are free of yolk. Use a whisk (either hand held or electric) and beat until the egg whites are stiff and form peaks when lifted with a spoon.

# Lemon Drizzle Cake

This is an absolutely fail safe recipe. It's a lovely, light teatime cake that also goes well with a tablespoon of virtually fat free fromage frais per person, for 1 additional **ProPoints** value per serving.

**Serves 10**

**low fat cooking spray**
**150 g tub low fat natural yogurt**
**175 g (6 oz) self raising flour**
**a pinch of salt**
**½ teaspoon baking powder**
**8 tablespoons artificial sweetener**
**75 ml (3 fl oz) sunflower oil**
**2 egg whites**

For the drizzle topping
**grated zest and juice of a lemon**
**2 tablespoons artificial sweetener**

---

**4 ProPoints** values per serving
**38 ProPoints** values per recipe

**150 calories** per serving

Takes **15 minutes** to prepare + cooling,
**45 minutes** to bake

V

\* recommended

1 Preheat the oven to Gas Mark 3/160°C/fan oven 140°C. Line an 18 cm (7 inch) cake tin with non stick baking parchment and spray it with the cooking spray. Mix all the cake ingredients, except the egg whites, together until smooth.

2 Beat the egg whites until they form stiff peaks then fold into the cake mixture and pour into the tin. Bake for 40–45 minutes. Check if it is cooked by inserting a thin skewer into the centre. If it comes out clean then the cake is cooked.

3 While the cake is cooking make the drizzle topping. Heat the lemon juice and zest in a small saucepan with the sweetener until the sweetener has dissolved.

4 When the cake is ready take it out of the oven, make holes with a skewer or fork all over the top and then pour the lemon juice mixture carefully over. Leave to cool before serving.

# Chocolate Mocha Fudge Cake

An indulgent cake or dessert with an intense flavour.

**Serves 12**

low fat cooking spray
175 g (6 oz) soft light brown sugar
2 eggs, plus 3 egg whites
100 g (3½ oz) self raising flour
15 g (½ oz) cocoa powder
½ teaspoon baking powder
a pinch of salt
100 g (3½ oz) instant dried polenta or cornmeal
275 g (9½ oz) low fat natural yogurt
1 teaspoon vanilla essence
25 g (1 oz) luxury dark chocolate (minimum 70% cocoa solids), grated
2 tablespoons instant coffee
2 tablespoons icing sugar
4 tablespoons boiling water

**For the frosting**

3 tablespoons icing sugar
2 tablespoons cocoa powder
1 teaspoon instant coffee
150 g (5½ oz) low fat soft cheese

**6 ProPoints** values per serving
**67 ProPoints** values per recipe

**202 calories** per serving

Takes **25 minutes** to prepare + cooling, **20 minutes** to bake

V

\*   recommended

1   Preheat the oven to Gas Mark 4/180°C/fan oven 160°C. Spray two 18 cm (7 inch) cake tins with the cooking spray and line them with baking parchment.

2   Beat the sugar with the 2 whole eggs for 2–3 minutes, using an electric whisk, until pale and thick. Sift the flour, cocoa, baking powder and salt over the egg mixture and beat in until smooth.

3   Stir in the polenta, yogurt, vanilla essence and half the grated chocolate (reserve the rest for the topping).

4   Clean the beaters thoroughly then, in a separate bowl, beat the egg whites until they form soft peaks. Stir a spoonful of beaten egg whites into the cake batter to loosen the mixture, then carefully fold in the remainder. Pour into the cake tins and level the surface.

5   Bake the sponges on the centre shelf for 20 minutes or until risen and firm.

6   Dissolve the coffee and icing sugar in the boiling water and drizzle this evenly over the sponges.

7   Cool the cakes in the tins for 10 minutes, then carefully remove from the tins and peel off the lining paper. Cool on a wire rack.

8   To make the frosting: sift the icing sugar and cocoa powder into a bowl. Stir in the instant coffee and beat together with the low fat soft cheese until smooth. Spread the frosting over both layers of cake, then stack one on top of the other. Sprinkle with the reserved grated chocolate.

# Stem Ginger Cake

This substantial and wonderfully chewy cake is great for picnics and lunch boxes. The stem ginger gives it a rich taste, which is complemented by the orange.

**Makes 16 slices**

low fat cooking spray
**175 g (6 oz) porridge oats**
**175 g (6 oz) self raising flour, sifted**
**75 g (2¾ oz) low fat spread**
**4 pieces stem ginger in syrup from a jar, drained and chopped**
**1 tablespoon syrup from the ginger jar**
**2 tablespoons ground ginger**
**6 tablespoons artificial sweetener**
**1 egg, beaten lightly**
**150 ml (5 fl oz) skimmed milk**
**grated zest and juice of an orange**

3 *ProPoints* values per serving
51 *ProPoints* values per recipe

**121 calories** per serving

Takes **10 minutes** to prepare + cooling,
**1 hour** to bake

V

*  recommended

1  Preheat the oven to Gas Mark 3/160°C/fan oven 140°C. Spray a 23 cm (9 inch) round springform cake tin with the cooking spray then line with baking parchment.

2  Combine the oats and flour in a bowl then rub in the low fat spread until the mixture resembles fine breadcrumbs. Stir in the stem ginger, syrup, ground ginger, sweetener, egg, milk, orange zest and juice.

3  Stir until all the ingredients have combined well and then pour into the tin. Bake for approximately 1 hour or until a skewer inserted into the centre comes out clean. Place the tin on a wire rack to cool completely before turning it out.

# Orchard Fruit and Ginger Teabread

**5 ProPoints value**

A slice of this lovely fruity teabread is perfect for a lunchbox or for the freezer. The dried apples and pears, together with a hint of ginger, give it a mildly spicy flavour.

**Makes 12 slices**

125 g (4½ oz) dried pears, chopped roughly
125 g (4½ oz) dried apples, chopped roughly
300 ml (10 fl oz) strong tea
225 g (8 oz) plain flour
2 teaspoons ground ginger
2 teaspoons baking powder
100 g (3½ oz) dark muscovado sugar
1 egg, beaten
25 g (1 oz) chopped stem ginger

**5 ProPoints** values per serving
**54 ProPoints** values per recipe

**155 calories** per serving

Takes **10 minutes** to prepare + soaking + cooling, **60 minutes** to bake

V

\* recommended

1 Cover the dried chopped fruit with the tea and leave to soak for 2 hours. Line a 900 g (2 lb) loaf tin with greaseproof paper or baking parchment.

2 Preheat the oven to Gas Mark 5/190°C/fan oven 170°C. Place all the ingredients in a large bowl and mix thoroughly. Turn into the prepared tin and level the surface. Bake for 55–60 minutes until firm. (Cover with a piece of greaseproof paper during cooking if the surface of the cake browns too quickly.)

3 Leave the cake to cool in the tin for 10 minutes before transferring to a wire rack.

**Tip** Look out for the wide variety of dried fruits now available. They are virtually fat free, naturally sweet and flavoursome, so they make an excellent cooking ingredient.

# White Chocolate and Raspberry Cake

This rich layered cake, sandwiched with fresh fruit, is perfect for a special occasion.

5 ProPoints value

**Serves 10**

low fat cooking spray

**For the sponge**

**100 g (3½ oz) low fat spread**
**100 g (3½ oz) caster sugar**
**175 g (6 oz) self raising flour, sifted**
**2 eggs**
**½ teaspoon vanilla extract**
**4 tablespoons skimmed milk**
**a pinch of salt**

**For the filling**

**50 g (1¾ oz) white cooking chocolate**
**150 g (5½ oz) low fat soft cheese**
**2 tablespoons icing sugar**
**200 g (7 oz) raspberries**

**5 *ProPoints*** values per serving
**55 *ProPoints*** values per recipe

**211 calories** per serving

Takes **20 minutes** to prepare + cooling,
**20 minutes** to bake

V

* recommended (  sponge)

1 Preheat the oven to Gas Mark 3/160°C/fan oven 140°C. Lightly spray two 18 cm (7 inch) cake tins with the cooking spray and line them with baking parchment.

2 Place all the sponge ingredients together in a mixing bowl and beat for 2–3 minutes, using an electric whisk, until pale and fluffy. Divide between the prepared cake tins and spread out evenly. Bake for 18–20 minutes until risen and springy to the touch. Turn out on to a wire rack to cool.

3 Use a vegetable peeler to make 10 g (¼ oz) white chocolate shavings to top the cake, and set aside in the fridge.

4 Break up the remaining chocolate and place in a heatproof bowl. Set over a pan of gently simmering water until melted. Cool slightly, then beat in the soft cheese and icing sugar until smooth. Chill in the fridge until needed.

5 To assemble the cake, spread half the white chocolate frosting over one layer of sponge and gently press in the raspberries. Top with the second sponge and spread the remaining frosting on top. Scatter the white chocolate shavings over the cake. Keep in the fridge until ready to serve.

# Squishy Squash Ginger Cake

The grated butternut squash keeps this sponge cake moist, while nuggets of stem ginger add little bursts of flavour.

**Serves 10**

**low fat cooking spray**
**200 g (7 oz) self raising flour**
**1 heaped teaspoon ground ginger**
**1 teaspoon baking powder**
**salt**
**100 g (3½ oz) soft light brown sugar**
**2 eggs, beaten**
**100 g (3½ oz) low fat spread, melted**
**2 tablespoons skimmed milk**
**40 g (1½ oz) stem ginger in syrup, drained and diced**
**175 g (6 oz) butternut squash, peeled, de-seeded and grated coarsely**
**15 g (½ oz) flaked almonds**

---

**5 ProPoints** values per serving
**48 ProPoints** values per recipe

**188 calories** per serving

Takes **20 minutes** to prepare + cooling, **45 minutes** to bake

V

✳ recommended

1 Preheat the oven to Gas Mark 4/180°C/fan oven 160°C. Lightly spray a 20 cm (8 inch) round deep cake tin with the cooking spray and line it with baking parchment.

2 Sift the flour, ginger, baking powder and a pinch of salt into a large bowl. Stir in the sugar then make a well in the centre. Add the beaten eggs, melted low fat spread and milk, then stir until smooth.

3 Mix in the diced ginger and grated squash, then pour into the prepared tin and level the surface. Scatter the flaked almonds on top.

4 Bake in the centre of the oven for 40–45 minutes, or until a skewer inserted into the centre comes out clean. Cover with baking parchment halfway through the cooking time if the cake is browning too quickly.

5 Cool the cake in the tin for 10 minutes before turning out on to a wire rack to finish cooling. Store in an airtight container.

**Cooking basics** To take the flesh from butternut squash: cut it in half and scoop out the seeds then either grate the flesh, as here, or cut into chunks and roast with some low fat cooking spray.

# Apple and Rosemary Cake

This is not an everyday cake, so share the delicious combination of flavours with friends and family.

**Serves 12**

**2 fresh rosemary sprigs**
**1 large cooking apple, peeled and grated**
**125 g (4½ oz) low fat spread**
**125 g (4½ oz) caster sugar**
**2 teaspoons vanilla essence**
**2 eggs, beaten**
**175 g (6 oz) self raising flour**
**2 tablespoons skimmed milk**

1 Preheat the oven to Gas Mark 4/180°C/fan oven 160°C. Line a 20 cm (8 inch) square cake tin with non stick baking parchment.

2 Remove the rosemary leaves from the stalks and chop finely. Toss with the grated apple.

3 Cream together the low fat spread and sugar until pale and fluffy. Add the vanilla essence and eggs along with 1 tablespoon of the flour and beat well. Sift in the remaining flour and stir in thoroughly with the grated apple and rosemary mixture and milk.

4 Spoon into a prepared tin and level with the back of a spoon. Bake for 50 minutes. Allow to cool in the tin for 20 minutes, then turn out on to a wire rack to cool completely. Cut into 12 fingers.

**4 *ProPoints*** values per serving
**46 *ProPoints*** values per recipe

C **149 calories** per serving

Takes **15 minutes** to prepare + cooling, **50 minutes** to bake

V

\* recommended.

**Tip** We normally associate rosemary with savoury dishes, especially lamb, but you'll be surprised to see how well it works with cakes too. However, use fresh, not dried, rosemary for the best results.

# Banana and Sultana Loaf

Another delicious fruit loaf for lunchboxes or teatime, using ripe bananas and store cupboard sultanas.

**Serves 16**

**low fat cooking spray**
**5 bananas, peeled**
**2 eggs, beaten**
**175 g (6 oz) soft brown sugar**
**100 g (3½ oz) sultanas**
**225 g (8 oz) wholemeal self raising flour**

1 Preheat the oven to Gas Mark 4/180°C/fan oven 160°C. Spray a 1 kg (2 lb 4 oz) loaf tin with the cooking spray and line with greaseproof paper.

2 Mash the bananas in a large mixing bowl and add the eggs, sugar and sultanas. Stir in the flour.

3 Transfer the mixture to the prepared tin and level the surface. Bake for 60–70 minutes, covering with foil halfway through. The loaf is ready when a skewer inserted into the centre of the cake comes out clean.

4 Cool in the tin for 10 minutes, then remove from the tin and cool on a wire rack.

**3 *ProPoints*** values per serving
**50 *ProPoints*** values per recipe

**150 calories** per serving

Takes **10 minutes** to prepare + cooling, **70 minutes** to bake

V

\* recommended

**Variation** You could also use the same quantity of white self raising flour. The ***ProPoints*** values per serving will remain the same.

**Tips** The cake is best when kept in an airtight tin for 24 hours before serving.

A potato masher is the ideal utensil for mashing the bananas; otherwise just use a fork.

# Raspberry and Apple Cake

This cake is delicious served warm or cool, either on its own or with 1 tablespoon of very low fat fromage frais per person, for an extra *ProPoints* value of 1 per serving.

**Serves 12**

low fat cooking spray
**225 g (8 oz) self raising flour**
**a pinch of salt**
**150 g (5½ oz) low fat spread**
**75 g (2¾ oz) caster sugar**
**225 g (8 oz) eating apples, peeled, cored and chopped**
**2 eggs, beaten**
**3 tablespoons skimmed milk**
**225 g (8 oz) fresh or frozen raspberries**
**25 g (1 oz) flaked almonds**
**1 teaspoon icing sugar, for dusting**

4 *ProPoints* values per serving
52 *ProPoints* values per recipe

174 **calories** per serving

Takes **20 minutes** to prepare,
**1¼ hours** to bake + cooling

V

* not recommended

1 Preheat the oven to Gas Mark 4/180°C/fan oven 160°C. Spray a 20 cm (8 inch) round springform cake tin with the cooking spray and line it with non stick baking parchment.

2 Sift the flour and salt into a large bowl. Rub in the low fat spread until the mixture resembles fresh breadcrumbs. Stir in the sugar and apples, then beat in the eggs and milk. Finally, gently fold in half the raspberries.

3 Spoon the mixture into the tin and level the surface, then sprinkle over the remaining raspberries and the flaked almonds. Bake for 1–1¼ hours or until well risen, golden brown and firm to the touch in the centre.

4 Remove from the tin and cool on a rack, then dust with icing sugar to serve.

**Tip** If you can't get fresh raspberries, frozen ones will work, so if you have some in the freezer, use these. Frozen fruit is great as a quick addition to smoothies too.

# Low Fat Sticky Gingerbread

You'll love this special low *ProPoints* value spicy gingerbread, which is always a teatime favourite.

**Makes 20 slices**

40 g (1½ oz) low fat spread
2 tablespoons marmalade
100 g (3½ oz) golden syrup
100 g (3½ oz) black treacle
50 g (1¾ oz) soft brown sugar
150 ml (50 fl oz) skimmed milk
low fat cooking spray
75 g (2¾ oz) wholemeal flour
75 g (2¾ oz) self raising flour
1 teaspoon ground ginger
1 teaspoon mixed spice
¼ teaspoon bicarbonate of soda
50 g (1¾ oz) porridge oats
1 large egg

3 *ProPoints* values per serving
55 *ProPoints* values per recipe

C  **94 calories** per serving

Takes **15 minutes** to prepare + cooling,
**1½ hours** to bake

V

✳  recommended

1  Put the low fat spread, marmalade, syrup, treacle and sugar into a large, heavy based saucepan and heat until bubbling, stirring well. Simmer gently for a few minutes until the sugar has completely dissolved. Remove from the heat and cool, then stir in the milk.

2  Preheat the oven to Gas Mark 2/150°C/fan oven 130°C. Spray an 18 cm (7 inch) square, deep cake tin with the cooking spray and line the base and sides with non stick baking parchment, cutting it to fit.

3  Put the flours, spices, bicarbonate of soda and the oats in a large bowl and stir well to mix.

4  When the mixture in the saucepan is cold, add the dry ingredients and the egg and beat until smooth. Pour this into the prepared tin.

5  Bake for 1¼ – 1½ hours until the cake has risen and is firm to the touch. Cool in the tin for half an hour, then turn out on to a wire rack and leave to cool completely. Peel off the baking parchment, wrap the cake in cling film and leave for at least a day so that it becomes nice and sticky. The gingerbread will keep for about a week.

# Golden Pumpkin Traybake

6 ProPoints value

A lovely, easy sponge, drizzled with orange icing.

**Makes 12**

40 g (1½ oz) dried apricots
a kettleful of boiling water
250 g (9 oz) pumpkin or butternut squash,
    peeled, de-seeded and cooked
low fat cooking spray
225 g (8 oz) self raising flour
1 teaspoon ground cinnamon (optional)
grated zest of an orange
200 g (7 oz) caster sugar
2 eggs, beaten
4 tablespoons vegetable oil

**For the icing**

75 g (2¾ oz) icing sugar
2 teaspoons fresh orange juice

---

6 *ProPoints* values per serving
72 *ProPoints* values per recipe

220 calories per serving

Takes **30 minutes** to prepare + soaking
+ cooling, **35 minutes** to bake

V

✳ recommended

1 Cover the apricots with boiling water and leave to plump up for 30 minutes. Drain, reserving 2 tablespoons of the liquid.

2 Place the pumpkin, or squash, and apricots in a food processor and purée to make 300 ml (10 fl oz), adding the reserved water if necessary.

3 Preheat the oven to Gas Mark 4/180°C/fan oven 160°C. Base line a 28 x 18 cm (11 x 7 inch) tin and lightly spray with the cooking spray.

4 Place the flour, cinnamon, if using, orange zest and sugar in a bowl and make a well in the centre. Add the eggs, oil and the purée and mix just enough to combine all the ingredients. Pour into the cake tin, levelling out the surface.

5 Bake for 30–35 minutes, until firm to the touch. Leave the cake to cool in the tin.

6 Meanwhile, make the icing. Mix together the icing sugar with just enough orange juice to make an icing that drizzles off the spoon. Using a teaspoon, drizzle the icing across the sponge surface. Leave to set before cutting into 12 pieces.

**Cooking basics** Preparing pumpkin: cut the pumpkin into wedges and then remove the flesh in large sections with a sharp knife. Alternatively, cut the pumpkin into strips and remove the rind with a potato peeler, before cutting into chunks. To cook, place the chunks in a steamer over a pan of simmering water for 10 minutes or until tender.

# Vanilla and Apricot Loaf

This is a moist and delicious treat that will keep in a cake tin for up to 4 days or freeze for up to 3 months. You can serve it warm as a pudding.

**Serves 10**

**125 ml (4 fl oz) sunflower oil**

**400 g can apricots in juice, drained and chopped roughly**

**1 vanilla pod, split and the seeds removed with the tip of a knife or 1 teaspoon vanilla extract**

**100 g (3½ oz) low fat natural yogurt**

**125 g (4½ oz) caster sugar**

**1 egg, beaten**

**175 g (6 oz) self raising flour, sifted**

**1 teaspoon icing sugar, for dusting**

6 *ProPoints* values per serving
65 *ProPoints* values per recipe

245 **calories** per serving

Takes **20 minutes** to prepare + cooling,
**50 minutes** to bake

V

✳ recommended

1 Preheat the oven to Gas Mark 4/180°C/fan oven 160°C and line a 900 g (2 lb) loaf tin with non stick baking parchment.

2 Put the oil, apricots, vanilla seeds or extract, yogurt, sugar, egg and flour in a large bowl and beat together until just smooth. Pour into the tin and bake for 45–50 minutes or until a skewer inserted in the centre comes out clean.

3 Turn the loaf out on to a cooling rack and then dust with icing sugar to serve.

**Store cupboard ideas** Keep a stock of flour, both self raising and plain. They come in handy for cakes or bakes; they're also good for thickening sauces.

# Courgette Tea Cake

The courgettes make this unusual cake lovely and moist.

**Serves 10**

**low fat cooking spray**
**75 g (2¾ oz) low fat spread**
**6 tablespoons artificial sweetener**
**450 g (1 lb) courgettes, grated**
**100 g (3½ oz) stoned dates, chopped**
**100 ml (3½ fl oz) orange juice**
**200 g (7 oz) self raising flour**
**½ teaspoon bicarbonate of soda**
**½ teaspoon salt**
**2 teaspoons cinnamon**
**½ teaspoon ground cloves**
**2 eggs, beaten**

---

**4 *ProPoints*** values per serving
**38 *ProPoints*** values per recipe

**195 calories** per serving

Takes **20 minutes** to prepare + cooling,
**30 minutes** to bake

V

\* not recommended

1 Preheat the oven to Gas Mark 4/180°C/fan oven 160°C. Spray a 1.2 litre (2 pint) loaf tin with the cooking spray and line it with baking parchment.

2 Cream together the low fat spread and sweetener until pale and fluffy.

3 Stir in the other ingredients. Tip into the prepared tin and bake for 30 minutes until well risen and just firm. If the top starts browning too much before the cake is cooked through, cover it with a piece of foil.

4 Leave in the tin until cool and then turn out on to a serving plate and slice to serve. This cake will keep in an airtight container for up to one week.

**Tip** This cake is made in a loaf tin and sliced like bread, but it can also be made in a 20 cm (8 inch) springform, round cake tin if you prefer.

# Carrot and Sultana Cake

A great cake for keeping – if you can resist it for long enough.

6 ProPoints value

## Makes 10 slices

low fat cooking spray
225 g (8 oz) plain flour
1 teaspoon baking powder
1 teaspoon bicarbonate of soda
1 teaspoon mixed spice
1 teaspoon salt
2 eggs, beaten
50 g (1¾ oz) dark muscovado sugar
3 tablespoons vegetable oil
2 tablespoons semi skimmed milk
juice of a large orange
300 g (10½ oz) carrots, peeled and grated
50 g (1¾ oz) sultanas

## For the frosting

225 g (8 oz) extra light low fat soft cheese
75 g (2¾ oz) virtually fat free fromage frais
4 tablespoons icing sugar, sifted
zest of an orange

---

6 *ProPoints* values per serving
62 *ProPoints* values per recipe

220 **calories** per serving

Takes **15 minutes** to prepare + cooling,
**65 minutes** to bake

V

✳ recommended for the cake only

1  Preheat the oven to Gas Mark 4/180°C/fan oven 160°C. Using baking parchment or greaseproof paper, base line a 20 cm (8 inch) round loose bottomed cake tin and lightly spray with the cooking spray.

2  Sift the flour, baking powder, bicarbonate of soda, mixed spice and salt into a mixing bowl. Make a well in the centre. Beat together the eggs, sugar, oil, milk and orange juice and pour into the centre. Mix together well to form a smooth batter. Beat in the carrots and sultanas.

3  Spoon the mixture into the tin. Bake for 55–65 minutes until a skewer comes out clean. Cool in the tin.

4  To make the frosting, beat the soft cheese with the fromage frais until soft and smooth. Beat in the icing sugar and the orange zest. Remove the cake from the tin and decorate with the frosting.

# Better Brownies

For a delicious treat at lunchtime, serve with a 60 g (2 oz) scoop of low fat vanilla ice cream per person, for an additional 2 **ProPoints** values per serving.

**Makes 12**

low fat cooking spray
75 g (2¾ oz) self raising flour
50 g (1¾ oz) unsweetened cocoa powder
¼ teaspoon salt
1 large egg
2 egg whites
175 g (6 oz) caster sugar
6 tablespoons unsweetened apple sauce
2 tablespoons sunflower oil
2 teaspoons vanilla essence
15 g (½ oz) chopped walnuts

---

4 **ProPoints** values per serving
47 **ProPoints** values per recipe

135 **calories** per serving

Takes **15 minutes** to prepare
+ **15 minutes** cooling, **25 minutes** to bake

V

✳ recommended

1  Preheat the oven to Gas Mark 4/180°C/fan oven 160°C. Spray a 20 cm (8 inch) square non stick baking pan with the cooking spray.

2  In a medium bowl, combine the flour, cocoa powder and salt, stirring together to mix.

3  In a large mixing bowl, whisk together the egg, egg whites, sugar, apple sauce, oil and vanilla essence.

4  Add the flour mixture to the egg mixture, stirring until just blended. Take care not to over mix, or the brownies will not rise.

5  Transfer the cake mixture to the baking pan and sprinkle with the walnuts.

6  Bake in the centre of the oven until just set – about 25 minutes. A toothpick or skewer inserted in the centre of the cake should come out clean.

7  Cool in the tin for 15 minutes, then cut into 12 rectangles.

**Tip** If you don't have a non stick cake pan, it is advisable to line your tin with greaseproof paper or baking parchment.

# Lemon and Ginger Roulade

Make a special occasion of teatime or dessert with this beautifully light and creamy sponge roll.

4 ProPoints value

**Serves 6**

**75 g (2¾ oz) caster sugar**
**3 eggs**
**75 g (2¾ oz) self raising flour**
**finely grated zest of a lemon**
**100 g (3½ oz) low fat soft cheese**
**4 tablespoons 0% fat Greek yogurt**
**15 g (½ oz) stem ginger, chopped finely**
**1 teaspoon icing sugar, for dusting**

4 *ProPoints* values per serving
27 *ProPoints* values per recipe

**171 calories** per serving

Takes **20 minutes** to prepare + cooling,
**15 minutes** to bake

V

✷ recommended

1 Preheat the oven to Gas Mark 6/200°C/fan oven 180°C. Line a Swiss roll tin with non stick baking parchment.

2 Using electric beaters, whisk together the caster sugar and eggs until very pale and fluffy. This will take about 5 minutes.

3 Sift the flour and carefully fold in with the lemon zest using a metal spoon.

4 Pour into the prepared tin. Bake for 12–15 minutes, until pale golden and springy.

5 Carefully turn out on to a clean sheet of baking parchment and peel away the lining paper. Using the clean paper as a guide, roll up the sponge and allow to cool.

6 Beat together the soft cheese, yogurt and stem ginger. Carefully unroll the cooled Swiss roll and spread with the ginger mixture. Roll up again, enclosing the filling, and dust the top with icing sugar before serving in slices.

# Hazelnut Cake

Make this luxurious cake, filled with chocolate mousse and pears, for a birthday or special anniversary.

**Makes 8 slices**

**3 egg whites**
**175 g (6 oz) caster sugar**
**1 teaspoon baking powder**
**100 g (3½ oz) ground hazelnuts**

**For the filling and decoration**

**2 x 55 g pots low calorie chocolate mousse**
**1 pear, peeled, cored and sliced thinly, or**
**200 g (7 oz) tinned pears in natural juice, drained**
**1 teaspoon icing sugar, to dust**

---

5 *ProPoints* values per serving
43 *ProPoints* values per recipe

201 **calories** per serving

Takes **20 minutes** to prepare + cooling,
**30 minutes** to bake

V

\* not recommended

1 Preheat the oven to Gas Mark 3/160°C/fan oven 140°C. Line two 18 cm (7 inch) non stick cake tins with non stick baking parchment.

2 Beat the egg whites until stiff then, using a metal spoon, gently mix in the sugar, baking powder and hazelnuts. Divide the mixture between the tins and bake for 30 minutes.

3 Carefully loosen the sides of the cakes with a knife and turn out on to a wire rack to cool.

4 When cool, carefully remove the baking parchment. Don't worry if a little cake comes away with the paper.

5 Just before serving, turn one cake upside down on a plate. Spread the chocolate mousse over it thinly and then layer the pear slices on top.

6 Place the second cake, top side uppermost, on top of the first and dust with the icing sugar.

# Petal Cakes

These pretty little cakes are fun to make and decorate – just the job for a party.

**Makes 12**

**125 g (4½ oz) caster sugar**
**125 g (4½ oz) low fat spread**
**125 g (4½ oz) self raising flour**
**2 large eggs, beaten**
**a pinch of salt**
**1 teaspoon vanilla essence**

For the decoration

**1 egg white**
**25 g (1 oz) caster sugar**
**12 tiny edible flowers, such as primroses,**
  **violets or rosebuds**
**25 g (1 oz) icing sugar**

**4 ProPoints** values per serving
**48 ProPoints** values per recipe

**149 calories** per serving

Takes **20 minutes** to prepare + cooling,
**20 minutes** to bake

V

* recommended before decorating.

1 Line a 12 hole patty tin with paper cake cases. Preheat the oven to Gas Mark 5/190°C/fan oven 170°C.

2 Put the sugar, low fat spread, flour, eggs, salt and vanilla essence into a large mixing bowl. Beat the mixture together vigorously with a wooden spoon for 1 minute.

3 Divide the mixture between the cake cases and bake for 18–20 minutes until risen and firm. Remove from the tin and allow to cool completely.

4 Meanwhile, make the crystallised flowers. Beat the egg white lightly and sprinkle the caster sugar on to a saucer. Paint the flower petals with the egg white and dip into the sugar. Allow the flowers to dry.

5 Mix the icing sugar with a little water to make a smooth glacé icing and spread on to the cakes. Decorate with the crystallised flowers (but do not eat the flowers unless you are sure they are edible).

**Tip** If you prefer, buy some crystallised violets or rose petals to save time decorating the cakes. Add the **ProPoints** values if necessary.

# Creamy Orange Gâteau

This gorgeous tiered cake is filled with creamy low fat fromage frais and tangy orange.

Serves 6

**low fat cooking spray**
**3 eggs, beaten**
**150 g (5½ oz) caster sugar**
**2 oranges**
**110 g (4 oz) plain flour**
**300 g (10½ oz) low fat plain fromage frais**

**6 ProPoints** values per serving
**36 ProPoints** values per recipe

C **250 calories** per serving

Takes **30 minutes** + cooling

V

\* not recommended

1 Preheat the oven to Gas Mark 6/200°C/fan oven 180°C. Spray two 20 cm (8 inch) cake tins with the cooking spray and line the base with non stick baking parchment.

2 Place the eggs in a large bowl with 110 g (4 oz) of the sugar and the finely grated zest of one of the oranges. Place the bowl over a pan of hot water and whisk until thick and foamy and the mixture leaves a trail. Sift over the flour and carefully fold in. Divide the mixture between the tins and bake for 10–12 minutes until golden and springy. Turn out on to a wire rack, remove the base lining and leave to cool.

3 Finely grate the zest of the remaining orange. Peel and segment both oranges, collecting any juice in a bowl. Put to one side. Mix together the zest, remaining sugar and fromage frais. Spread half the fromage frais mixture over one cake and scatter with half the orange segments. Top it with the other cake and spread over the remaining fromage frais. Serve sliced, with the remaining orange segments and juice. Store in the fridge.

# Lemon Madeleines

A favourite in France and Spain, these little shell shaped cakes will delight any time.

Makes 24

**low fat cooking spray**
**125 g (4½ oz) caster sugar**
**4 eggs**
**finely grated zest of 2 lemons**
**125 g (4½ oz) plain flour**
**1 teaspoon baking powder**
**a pinch of salt**
**100 g (3½ oz) butter, melted and cooled**
**2 teaspoons icing sugar, for dusting**

2 *ProPoints* values per serving
56 *ProPoints* values per recipe

86 **calories** per serving

Takes **30 minutes** + **40 minutes** chilling + cooling

V

✳ recommended

1 Lightly spray two trays of madeleine moulds with the cooking spray.

2 In a large bowl, whisk together the caster sugar, eggs and lemon zest until pale, fluffy and thick enough to leave a trail when the whisk is lifted.

3 Sift in half the flour with the baking powder and the salt. Drizzle half the butter over and then carefully fold in using a metal spoon. Repeat with the remaining flour and butter. Cover and chill for 40 minutes.

4 Preheat the oven to Gas Mark 7/220°C/fan oven 200°C.

5 Fill the prepared moulds two thirds full with the mixture and bake for 10 minutes until well risen, golden and springy to the touch.

6 Carefully remove the madeleines from the moulds and transfer to a wire rack to cool. Dust with icing sugar before serving.

# Snow Covered Christmas Cake

**9 ProPoints value**

This traditional Christmas cake makes a beautiful centrepiece for your Christmas tea.

Serves 18

**550 g (1 lb 3 oz) dried luxury mixed fruit**
**100 g (3½ oz) glacé cherries, halved**
**100 g (3½ oz) chopped mixed nuts**
**juice and finely grated zest of an orange**
**3 tablespoons brandy (or use more orange juice)**
**low fat cooking spray**
**225 g (8 oz) low fat spread**
**200 g (7 oz) soft brown sugar**
**5 eggs**
**250 g (9 oz) plain flour**
**2 teaspoons ground mixed spice or cinnamon**

For the icing

**2 tablespoons low calorie apricot jam**
**75 g (2¾ oz) icing sugar, sifted**

**9 ProPoints** values per serving
**161 ProPoints** values per recipe

C **326 calories** per serving

Takes **30 minutes** to prepare + overnight soaking, **2¼ hours** to bake + **1 hour** cooling + setting

V

\* recommended without icing (ice when defrosted)

1 Mix the first five ingredients together in a bowl and leave, preferably overnight, to soak.

2 Preheat the oven to Gas Mark 2/150°C/fan oven 130°C. Spray a 22 x 9 cm (8½ x 3½ inch) ring tin or a 20 cm (8 inch) round cake tin with the cooking spray.

3 Cream the low fat spread and sugar together until light and fluffy, preferably with an electric whisk. Then beat in the eggs one at a time.

4 Sift the flour and mixed spice and lightly fold into the mixture. Then fold in the fruit mixture and make a batter just moist enough to drop off the spoon.

5 Spoon into the prepared tin and tie a double layer of baking parchment around it. Bake for about 2¼ hours or until a warm skewer inserted into the middle comes out clean. Cover the cake in the last hour if it is becoming too brown.

6 Allow the cake to cool in the tin for an hour before placing on a cooling rack. To keep, wrap in greaseproof paper and then a layer of foil when it has cooled completely.

7 To ice, place the cooled cake on a board and warm the jam in a saucepan with 2 tablespoons of water until melted. Brush the cake with the jam.

8 Mix the icing sugar with just enough boiling water to make a smooth, slightly runny mixture (about 2 tablespoons). Drizzle over the top of the cake, allowing it to run down the sides, and then leave to set.

# Triple Decker Lime Cream Sponge

5 ProPoints value

This impressive three tiered sponge cake is made with low fat yogurt, Quark and soft cheese, as well as lemon curd, for a wonderfully rich and creamy filling.

**Makes 8 slices**

low fat cooking spray
4 eggs
100 g (3½ oz) golden caster sugar
100 g (3½ oz) self raising flour
150 g (5½ oz) Quark
75 g (2¾ oz) 0% fat Greek yogurt
100 g (3½ oz) low fat soft cheese
½ tablespoon artificial sweetener
grated zest of 2 limes
1½ tablespoons lime juice
4 teaspoons lemon curd
1 drop green food colouring (optional)
mint leaves, to garnish (optional)
½ teaspoon icing sugar, to dust

**5 ProPoints** values per serving
**37 ProPoints** values per recipe

**184 calories** per serving

Takes **15 minutes** to prepare, **15 minutes** to bake + **30 minutes** chilling

V

\* recommended (sponges only)

1 Line three 18 cm (7 inch) sandwich cake tins with baking parchment sprayed with the cooking spray. Preheat the oven to Gas Mark 4/180°C/fan oven 160°C.

2 Fill a heavy bowl or pan with hot (not boiling) water and place another bowl on top of it. The bottom of the top bowl should not touch the water. Break the eggs into the bowl and, using an electric beater, whisk for a minute. Add the sugar and whisk for a further 3 minutes or until the mixture has doubled in size, has a soft meringue consistency and is a very light colour. Remove the pan and water and continue to whisk for another minute to cool the mixture a little. (If you don't have an electric beater, expect to spend around 15 minutes to create the same volume with a hand whisk.)

3 Gently fold in the flour with a large metal spoon and transfer to the three prepared cake tins. Bake for 10–15 minutes or until golden and well risen. Turn out on to a cooling rack. When cool, remove the baking parchment.

4 Meanwhile, beat together all the remaining ingredients except the mint leaves and icing sugar, and check that the sweetness is to your taste. Add a little more sweetener (or a ½ tablespoon more lime juice) if you like. Chill the filling in the fridge for at least 30 minutes.

5 Once everything is cool, select the best looking cake to go on top and then spread the filling over the other two pieces and sandwich all three together. Decorate by topping with the mint leaves (if using), and dusting with the icing sugar. Cut into eight slices.

# Carrot and Pineapple Squares

Tempting squares of luscious frosted carrot and pineapple cake. Individual pieces can be wrapped in cling film and frozen if you wish.

**Makes 15**

**low fat cooking spray**
**3 eggs**
**100 g (3½ oz) caster sugar**
**80 g (3 oz) low fat spread, melted**
**200 g (7 oz) self raising flour**
**2 teaspoons mixed spice**
**salt**
**250 g (9 oz) carrots, peeled and grated coarsely**
**432 g can crushed pineapple, well drained**

For the frosting
**100 g (3½ oz) low fat soft cheese**
**60 g (2 oz) very low fat plain fromage frais**
**1 tablespoon icing sugar, sifted**
**¼ teaspoon mixed spice**

3 *ProPoints* values per serving
48 *ProPoints* values per recipe

135 **calories** per serving

Takes **20 minutes** to prepare + cooling,
**30 minutes** to bake

V

✳ recommended

1  Preheat the oven to Gas Mark 4/180°C/fan oven 160°C.

2  Lightly spray an 18 x 28 cm (7 x 11 inch) rectangular baking tin with the cooking spray and line it with baking parchment.

3  Beat the eggs and sugar with an electric whisk until creamy and thick. Pour in the melted low fat spread, then sift in the flour, mixed spice and a pinch of salt.

4  Fold in to give a smooth batter, then stir in the grated carrots and drained pineapple.

5  Spoon into the prepared tin and then smooth the top. Bake on the centre shelf of the oven for 25–30 minutes until the cake is risen and firm to the touch. Turn out and cool on a wire rack.

6  To make the frosting, beat the soft cheese with the fromage frais and icing sugar until smooth. Spread evenly over the cooled cake and dust with the mixed spice.

7  Cut into squares, and store in an airtight container in the fridge for up to 3 days.

# Biscuits, Bread and Bakes

One of the best things in life is the aroma of fresh baking. The feeling when you take a tray of home made biscuits, scones or muffins, beautifully warm and risen, out of the oven is second to none. Try these delicious recipes, including Fruit Scones, Cheese and Tomato Muffins, Cinnamon Cookies and Mediterranean Bread. Make them as a treat at teatime, or perhaps to accompany a light lunch.

Soft and crumbly, warm from the oven – this is beautiful baking

# Banana Oat Bars

Grab one of these for breakfast on the run.

**Makes 10**

**low fat cooking spray**
**100 g (3½ oz) porridge oats**
**2 tablespoons artificial sweetener**
**½ teaspoon cream of tartar**
**½ teaspoon ground cinnamon**
**3 ripe bananas, mashed**
**2 eggs, separated**
**150 g (5½ oz) low fat natural yogurt**

**2** *ProPoints* values per serving
**16** *ProPoints* values per recipe

**99 calories** per serving

Takes **15 minutes** to prepare + cooling,
**30 minutes** to bake

V

❋ recommended

1 Preheat the oven to Gas Mark 4/180°C/fan oven 160°C. Lightly spray a 20 cm (8 inch) square cake tin with the cooking spray and line it with baking parchment.

2 Reserve 1 tablespoon of oats to top the bars, then whizz the rest to a powder in a food processor.

3 Mix with the sweetener, cream of tartar and cinnamon, then add the mashed bananas, egg yolks and yogurt.

4 In a separate bowl, whisk the egg whites to soft peaks. Stir a spoonful into the banana oat batter to loosen it, then carefully fold in the remainder.

5 Pour into the prepared tin and scatter with the reserved oats.

6 Bake on the centre shelf of the oven for 30 minutes until firm and springy. Cool in the tin then set on a wire rack.

7 Cut into 10 fingers and store in an airtight container, or wrap individual bars in cling film and freeze.

# Blueberry Cookies

These gorgeous little cookies should be served in true American style with a glass of skimmed milk. The uncooked cookie dough can be wrapped in cling film and frozen for up to three months.

**Makes 12 cookies**

75 g (2¾ oz) low fat spread
5 tablespoons artificial sweetener
1 egg, beaten
½ teaspoon vanilla essence
a pinch of salt
175 g (6 oz) self raising flour, sifted
grated zest of a lemon
150 g (5½ oz) fresh blueberries

2 *ProPoints* values per serving
25 *ProPoints* values per recipe

83 **calories** per serving

Takes **15 minutes** to prepare + cooling,
**15 minutes** to bake

V

\* recommended (dough only)

1 Preheat the oven to Gas Mark 4/180°C/fan oven 160°C and line two baking trays with baking parchment.

2 Cream together the low fat spread and sweetener until light and fluffy, then add the egg and vanilla essence and beat again. Add the salt, flour and lemon zest. Stir together until you have a smooth dough.

3 Place tablespoons of the dough on to the baking trays, spaced well apart, and shape each one into a round. Press the blueberries into the top of the cookies and bake for 12–15 minutes, until golden. Cool on a wire rack.

**Tip** Use vanilla essence (or extract), rather than vanilla flavouring, which may smell like vanilla, but is nothing like the real thing.

# Nutmeg and Yogurt Scone Squares ③

When friends or family arrive unexpectedly, surprise them with these super speedy scones.

**225 g (8 oz) self raising white flour, plus
    1 tablespoon for rolling**
**½ teaspoon ground nutmeg**
**¼ teaspoon salt**
**25 g (1 oz) low fat spread**
**25 g (1 oz) caster sugar**
**150 ml (5 fl oz) low fat natural yogurt**
**1 tablespoon skimmed milk**

**3 *ProPoints*** values per serving
**28 *ProPoints*** values per recipe

**117 calories** per serving

Takes **15 minutes** to prepare + cooling,
**15 minutes** to bake

V

\* recommended

1 Preheat the oven to Gas Mark 6/200°C/fan oven 180°C. Line a baking tray with non stick baking parchment.

2 Sift the flour into a mixing bowl with the nutmeg and salt. Rub in the low fat spread, using your fingertips, until the mixture resembles fine breadcrumbs. Stir in the sugar and then make a well in the centre. Place the yogurt in the well and then mix it all to form a soft dough.

3 Sprinkle a clean work surface with the extra flour. Roll out the dough to a 23 cm (9 inch) square. Cut the square into nine smaller squares. Place each square on the lined baking tray and brush the tops with skimmed milk.

4 Bake for 12–15 minutes until well risen and golden.

**Tip** These are delicious split and served with a heaped teaspoon of low calorie jam, for 1 additional ***ProPoints*** value per serving.

# Saffron Scones

Saffron may be expensive but you only need a tiny bit to colour and flavour these extra special scones.

**Makes 26 small scones**

**low fat cooking spray**
**225 g (8 oz) self raising flour**
**¼ teaspoon salt**
**40 g (1½ oz) low fat spread**
**150 ml (5 fl oz) skimmed milk**
**a pinch of strands of saffron, soaked in**
**  2 tablespoons boiling water**

**1** *ProPoints* value per serving
**25** *ProPoints* values per recipe

**36 calories** per serving

Takes **15 minutes** to prepare + cooling,
**15 minutes** to bake

V

✱  recommended

1 Preheat the oven to Gas Mark 7/220°C/fan oven 200°C. Spray a baking tray with the cooking spray and then line with baking parchment.

2 Sift the flour into a large bowl with the salt. Cut the low fat spread into small pieces and add to the bowl. Rub the flour and low fat spread together with your fingertips until the mixture resembles fine breadcrumbs.

3 Make a well in the centre of the flour mixture. Pour in all but 2 tablespoons of the milk, and the saffron and its soaking water. Gradually stir into the mixture. Turn out on to a floured surface and knead very quickly and lightly to form a smooth dough.

4 Press out the dough gently with the palms of your hands to about 1 cm (½ inch) thick. Using a cutter, cut rounds about 2.5 cm (1 inch) in diameter. Place on the prepared baking tray. Press together the trimmings and repeat the rolling and cutting process until all the dough is used up.

5 Brush the tops of the unbaked scones with a little milk and bake for 12–15 minutes until risen and golden. Cool on a wire rack until you are ready to eat. Serve warm.

# Fruit Scones

These great little scones come with their own portion of jam already spread inside.

2 ProPoints value

Makes 12 scones

**200 g (7 oz) self raising flour, plus 1 tablespoon for rolling**
**½ teaspoon salt**
**40 g (1½ oz) low fat spread**
**25 g (1 oz) caster sugar**
**100 ml (3½ fl oz) buttermilk**
**4 tablespoons skimmed milk**
**100 g (3½ oz) raspberries or blackberries (or a mixture of both), cut into small pieces**

**2 ProPoints** values per serving
**27 ProPoints** values per recipe

**84 calories** per serving.

Takes **25 minutes**

V

\* not recommended

1 Preheat the oven to Gas Mark 7/220°C/fan oven 200°C.

2 Sift the flour and salt into a bowl and rub in the low fat spread until the mixture resembles fine breadcrumbs. Stir in the sugar.

3 Whisk the buttermilk and skimmed milk together thoroughly in a jug. Add about three quarters of this to the dry ingredients and mix well with a palette knife. Your aim is to add just enough milk to make the dough soft, but it should not stick to your hands. If you need a little more milk, add a tablespoon at a time until you reach this consistency. Knead the dough briefly in the bowl to ensure everything is well combined.

4 Sprinkle a work surface with the reserved flour and roll out the dough to a thickness of 5 mm (¼ inch). Using a 5 cm (2 inch) pastry cutter, cut 24 circles from the dough and place half of them on a non stick baking tray. Brush the edges with some of the remaining buttermilk mixture. Divide the fruit between the circles, placing it towards the centre of each one. Top with the remaining circles of dough and gently squash them down to seal the fruit inside the scone.

5 Brush again with the remaining buttermilk mixture and bake in the oven for 12 minutes or until risen and golden brown. Serve with the topping of your choice (see below).

**Variations** Select your toppings and add the appropriate **ProPoints** values:

1 teaspoon butter = **ProPoints** value: 1

1 teaspoon low fat spread = **ProPoints** value: 1

1 tablespoon clotted cream = **ProPoints** values: 3

1 tablespoon whipped cream = **ProPoints** values: 2

# Olive and Tomato Rolls with Basil

7 ProPoints value

There's nothing like the smell of fresh bread cooking in your home, and it tastes so wonderful too.

**Serves 12**

50 g (1¾ oz) sun-dried tomatoes
425 ml (15 fl oz) boiling water
1 teaspoon caster sugar
1 tablespoon easy blend dried yeast
700 g (1 lb 9 oz) strong white bread flour
2 teaspoons salt
75 g (2¾ oz) pitted black olives, diced
3 tablespoons torn fresh basil
1 tablespoon olive oil

7 *ProPoints* values per serving
80 *ProPoints* values per recipe

**220 calories** per serving

Takes **30 minutes** to prepare +
standing, rising and cooling time,
**20 minutes** to bake

V

✳ recommended

1 Place the sun-dried tomatoes in a small bowl. Cover with the boiled water and leave to stand for 15 minutes. Drain, reserving the liquid and then dice the tomatoes.

2 Stir the sugar into the reserved water and then place the yeast, flour and salt in a large warmed mixing bowl. Stir well. Add the reserved soaking liquid and mix to a soft dough.

3 Turn out on to a lightly floured surface and knead for 5 minutes until smooth and elastic. Place in a clean, lightly oiled bowl. Cover with a damp tea towel and leave to rise in a warm place until doubled in size.

4 Turn out on to a clean surface and knock out the air. Work in the chopped tomatoes, olives and basil by kneading them in. Divide the mixture into small rolls and lift on to a lightly oiled baking tray. Cover with a damp tea towel and leave to rise in a warm place for 20 minutes. Brush the tops with any remaining oil and bake for 20 minutes until well risen and golden.

5 Allow the rolls to cool for at least 30 minutes before serving.

**Variation:** You may wish to make two large loaves instead of small buns. Shape the dough into two rounds and then bake for 25–30 minutes.

# Strawberry Shortcakes

An American style dessert of freshly baked sweet scones with a creamy filling and fresh berries.

Serves 6

**225 g (8 oz) self raising flour**
**a pinch of salt**
**25 g (1 oz) low fat spread**
**25 g (1 oz) caster sugar**
**300 g (10½ oz) very low fat plain fromage frais**
**6 heaped teaspoons low sugar strawberry jam**
**110 g (4 oz) strawberries, sliced**

**5 ProPoints** values per serving
**32 ProPoints** values per recipe

**203 calories** per serving

Takes **25 minutes** + cooling

V

✻ recommended (unfilled shortcakes only)

1 Preheat the oven to Gas Mark 7/220°C/fan oven 200°C.

2 Reserve 2 teaspoons of flour for rolling out, then sift the rest into a mixing bowl with a pinch of salt. Rub in the low fat spread until the mixture looks like breadcrumbs then stir in all but 1 teaspoon of the sugar (keep this for the tops).

3 Mix in 200 g (7 oz) of the fromage frais, with a knife, to make a soft, but not sticky, dough. Add a little water if needed.

4 Pat the dough out on a floured work surface, to a depth of 2 cm (¾ inch), then use a floured 6 cm (2½ inch) cutter to stamp out six rounds. Transfer to a baking tray, brush the tops of the shortcakes with water and sprinkle with the reserved sugar. Bake for 10–12 minutes until risen and golden.

5 Meanwhile, stir the strawberry jam into the remaining fromage frais. Cool the shortcakes for a few minutes then split and top with the fromage frais mixture and strawberries.

# Cheese and Tomato Muffins

If you find 12 of these too tempting, the recipe halves easily, and the muffins also freeze really well.

**Makes 12 large muffins**

110 g (4 oz) self raising flour
225 g (8 oz) cornmeal
1 teaspoon dried mustard powder
1 tablespoon baking powder
100 g (3½ oz) semi-dried tomatoes, soaked, drained and chopped roughly
1 teaspoon salt
100 g (3½ oz) half fat Cheddar cheese, grated
2 eggs
50 ml (2 fl oz) mild or delicate flavoured olive oil
4 tablespoons low fat natural yogurt
300 ml (10 fl oz) skimmed milk

**5 ProPoints** values per serving
**64 ProPoints** values per recipe

**195 calories** per serving

Takes **10 minutes** to prepare + cooling, **20 minutes** to bake

V

✳ recommended

1 Preheat the oven to Gas Mark 6/200°C/fan oven 180°C and line a 12 hole muffin tin with paper muffin cases.

2 Sift together the flour, cornmeal, mustard powder and baking powder. Stir in the tomatoes, salt and 75 g (2¾ oz) of the grated cheese.

3 In another bowl, beat the eggs with the oil, yogurt and milk and then pour this into the dry ingredients and mix until just combined. Divide the mixture between the baking cases and top the muffins with the remaining cheese.

4 Bake for 20 minutes, or until the muffins are golden and well risen. They are best left to cool as they will then come out of their wrappers more easily and the flavour of the cheese will be stronger.

**Tip** Cornmeal is sometimes called maize meal and is readily available in larger supermarkets and health food shops.

# Marmalade Muffins

These muffins are delicious for breakfast, afternoon tea or in a lunchbox.

**Makes 10 muffins**

**150 g (5½ oz) self raising flour**
**¼ teaspoon baking powder**
**2 tablespoons artificial sweetener**
**1 egg, beaten**
**50 g (1¾ oz) low fat natural yogurt**
**juice of ½ a large orange**
**5 tablespoons reduced sugar orange jam**
  **or marmalade**
**50 g (1¾ oz) low fat spread, melted**

---

**3 ProPoints** values per serving
**29 ProPoints** values per recipe

**111 calories** per serving

Takes **10 minutes** to prepare + cooling,
**25 minutes** to bake

V

✳ recommended (reheat to serve)

1 Preheat the oven to Gas Mark 5/190°C/fan oven 170°C. Place 10 paper cases in a muffin tin. Mix the flour, baking powder and sweetener together in a large bowl.

2 Beat the egg, yogurt, orange juice, jam or marmalade and melted low fat spread together in a smaller bowl.

3 Gently stir the wet ingredients into the dry (see Tip) and then quickly spoon into the muffin cases. Bake the muffins for 25 minutes or until they are well risen and golden on top.

4 Remove from the oven and allow to cool in the tin for 5 minutes before transferring to a wire rack.

**Tip** It's best to use a very light and quick hand to mix muffins – stop after a maximum of 10 stirs. Lumps in the mixture do not matter; in fact they signify the lightness to come.

# Cranberry Muffins

Ring the changes by using dried cranberries from your store cupboard for these delicious muffins.

**Makes 12**

**300 g (10½ oz) plain flour**
**2 teaspoons baking powder**
**½ teaspoon ground cinnamon**
**150 g (5½ oz) light muscovado sugar**
**50 g (1¾ oz) dried cranberries**
**1 egg**
**225 ml (8 fl oz) skimmed milk**
**50 ml (2 fl oz) sunflower oil**

**6 *ProPoints*** values per serving
**67 *ProPoints*** values per recipe

**200 calories** per serving

Takes **15 minutes** to prepare + cooling,
**20 minutes** to bake

V

✳ recommended

1 Line a 12 case muffin tray with paper muffin cases. Preheat the oven to Gas Mark 6/200°C/fan oven 180°C.

2 Sift the flour, baking powder and cinnamon into a mixing bowl. Stir in the sugar and cranberries.

3 Beat together the egg, milk and oil and add to the dry ingredients. Mix well to a dropping consistency.

4 Spoon the mixture into the muffin cases and bake for 15–20 minutes, until well risen and just firm. Transfer to a cooling rack to cool a little before serving.

**Variation** As an alternative, use sultanas instead of dried cranberries and flavour with lemon or orange zest instead of cinnamon. The *ProPoints* values per serving will be the same.

# Must Have Muffins

These muffins are perfect to satisfy a savoury craving.

**5** ProPoints value

**Makes 12**

**low fat cooking spray**
**1 large onion, chopped finely**
**100 g (3½ oz) smoked or unsmoked**
   **turkey rashers, chopped finely**
**300 g (10½ oz) plain flour**
**1 teaspoon salt**
**1 teaspoon paprika**
**4 teaspoons baking powder**
**75 g (2¾ oz) low fat spread**
**150 g (5½ oz) half fat mature Cheddar**
   **cheese, grated**
**1 egg**
**200 ml (7 fl oz) skimmed milk**

**5** *ProPoints* values per serving
**54** *ProPoints* values per recipe

**167 calories** per serving

Takes **20 minutes** to prepare + cooling,
**20 minutes** to bake

✳ recommended

1 Preheat the oven to Gas Mark 5/190°C/fan oven 170°C. Spray a 12 hole muffin tin with the cooking spray.

2 Spray a medium, non stick frying pan with the cooking spray and heat for a few moments. Add the onion and cook for 2–3 minutes, then add the chopped turkey rashers and cook, stirring, for another 2 minutes. Remove from the heat to cool.

3 Put the flour, salt, paprika and baking powder into a mixing bowl. Stir well. Add the low fat spread and rub in, using your fingertips, until the mixture resembles fine breadcrumbs.

4 Stir in the cooled onion and turkey mixture and half the grated cheese. Mix the egg and milk together, then add to the mixing bowl and stir until just combined.

5 Spoon the mixture into the prepared muffin tins and sprinkle with the remaining cheese.

6 Bake for 20 minutes until risen and golden brown. Cool on a wire rack.

**Tip** Make sure that you use proper cook's measuring spoons. This is vital when measuring baking powder; level off the surface with a knife for an accurate amount.

**Variation** Add a tablespoon of chopped fresh herbs, such as chives or parsley to the mixture. Or try a teaspoon of mixed dried herbs instead.

# Banana Muffins

These are gorgeous for breakfast, served with honey or marmalade. Add 1 *ProPoints* value per heaped teaspoon.

**Makes 12**

250 g (9 oz) plain flour
1 teaspoon baking powder
1 teaspoon bicarbonate of soda
½ teaspoon salt
1 egg, beaten
80 g (3 oz) soft brown sugar
3 well ripened bananas, peeled and mashed
  to a purée
4 tablespoons corn oil

4 *ProPoints* values per serving
50 *ProPoints* values per recipe

C  **180 calories** per serving

Takes **15 minutes** to prepare + cooling,
**25 minutes** to bake

V

✳ recommended

1 Preheat the oven to Gas Mark 5/190°C/fan oven 170°C.

2 Put 12 paper cases in suitable muffin tins.

3 Sift together the flour, baking powder, bicarbonate of soda and salt.

4 In another bowl, beat together the egg, 5 tablespoons of water, sugar and bananas.

5 Add the corn oil to the wet ingredients and stir well.

6 Quickly combine the two sets of ingredients and mix just enough to combine – you should have a lumpy consistency.

7 Spoon the mixture into the paper cases and bake for 20–25 minutes, until firm and springy.

8 Cool on a rack.

# Apple and Apricot Muffins

If you're short of time in the morning and need to grab breakfast on the run, make sure you've got a batch of these muffins stored in the freezer.

**Makes 12 muffins**

**low fat cooking spray**
**grated zest and juice of ½ a lemon**
**200 ml (7 fl oz) skimmed milk**
**300 g (10½ oz) self raising flour, sifted**
**1 teaspoon baking powder**
**salt**
**60 g (2 oz) caster sugar**
**100 g (3½ oz) dried apricots, chopped**
**1 apple, cored and diced**
**1 egg, beaten**
**80 g (3 oz) low fat spread**

4 *ProPoints* values per serving
50 *ProPoints* values per recipe

**158 calories** per serving

Takes **10 minutes** to prepare + cooling,
**25 minutes** to bake

V

✳ recommended

1 Preheat the oven to Gas Mark 6/200°C/fan oven 180°C.

2 Lightly spray a 12 hole muffin tin with the cooking spray, or line with paper muffin cases.

3 Mix the lemon juice into the milk and set aside for 5 minutes to curdle. This will give the muffins a lovely light texture.

4 Sift the flour, baking powder and a pinch of salt into a mixing bowl. Stir in the sugar, lemon zest, dried apricots and apple, then make a well in the centre.

5 Pour the milk, egg and melted low fat spread into the bowl then stir briefly to mix into a batter. The batter should still look slightly lumpy; if you overwork the mixture the muffins will be tough. Spoon into the muffin tin or paper cases then bake for 20–25 minutes until the muffins are well risen, firm and golden brown. Cool on a wire rack.

# Fresh Blackberry Muffins

Pick your own blackberries from the autumn hedgerows if you can as they have an unbeatable taste.

**Makes 12 muffins**

**200 g (7 oz) plain flour**
**½ teaspoon bicarbonate of soda**
**2 teaspoons baking powder**
**6 tablespoons artificial sweetener**
**a pinch of salt**
**75 g (2¾ oz) low fat spread, melted**
**100 g (3½ oz) low fat natural yogurt**
**100 ml (3½ fl oz) skimmed milk**
**1 egg**
**200 g (7 oz) fresh blackberries**

**3 *ProPoints*** values per serving
**32 *ProPoints*** values per recipe

**104 calories** per serving

Takes **15 minutes** to prepare + cooling,
**20 minutes** to bake

V

✳ recommended

1 Preheat the oven to Gas Mark 6/200°C/fan oven 180°C. Line a patty tin or muffin tray with 12 paper cases.

2 Combine all the dry ingredients in a bowl. Separately beat the melted low fat spread, yogurt, milk and egg together in a measuring jug.

3 Pour the wet ingredients into the dry and, using a light hand as it's important not to overwork the mixture, mix gently to combine.

4 Stir in the blackberries, again keeping the mixing to a minimum, and then quickly spoon into the paper cases. Bake for 20 minutes, until risen and golden on top.

5 Transfer to a wire rack and cool, or eat warm. Store in an airtight container for up to three days.

# Raisin and Honey Flapjacks

Full of goodness, these chewy flapjacks are great in a lunchbox.

**Makes 10 flapjacks**

**125 g (4½ oz) low fat spread**
**125 g (4½ oz) demerara sugar**
**3 tablespoons clear honey**
**50 g (1¾ oz) raisins**
**1 teaspoon ground mixed spice**
**200 g (7 oz) rolled oats**

**6 *ProPoints*** values per serving
**57 *ProPoints*** values per recipe

**186 calories** per serving

Takes **10 minutes** to prepare,
**20 minutes** to bake

V

✳ not recommended

1 Preheat the oven to Gas Mark 5/190°C/fan oven 170°C. Line a 20 cm (8 inch) non stick square baking tin with non stick baking parchment.

2 Place the low fat spread, sugar and honey in a small saucepan and heat gently until dissolved.

3 Mix in the raisins, mixed spice and rolled oats. Press the mixture into the prepared tin and level with the back of a metal spoon. Bake for 20 minutes.

4 Mark out 10 fingers while the flapjack is still warm.

**Tip** Flapjacks should have a soft, chewy texture so take care not to overcook them, or they will become brittle.

# Going for Gold

These impressive scones, with cherries on top, are so quick to make.

**Serves 16**

**100 g (3½ oz) wholemeal self raising flour**
**100 g (3½ oz) white self raising flour**
**50 g (1¾ oz) low fat spread**
**25 g (1 oz) glacé cherries, chopped**
**25 g (1 oz) caster sugar**
**1 egg**
**450 ml (16 fl oz) skimmed milk**
**8 glacé cherries, halved**

2 *ProPoints* values per serving
34 *ProPoints* values per recipe

75 **calories** per serving

Takes **15 minutes** to prepare,
**15 minutes** to bake

V

\* recommended

1 Preheat the oven to Gas Mark 6/200°C/fan oven 180°C.

2 Put the two types of flour in a mixing bowl and mix them together. Add the low fat spread and rub in, using your fingertips, until the mixture resembles fine breadcrumbs.

3 Add the chopped cherries and sugar to the rubbed in mixture. Beat the egg and milk together, then add just enough to the mixture to make a soft, but not sticky, dough. Knead lightly on a work surface sprinkled with a little flour for a few moments, until smooth.

4 Divide the mixture into four equal pieces and roll each piece into a ball. Flatten out with your hand to a thickness of 1 cm (½ inch). Place on lightly greased baking trays and cut a deep cross into each one, to divide into four. Brush with the remaining egg mixture. Top each section with a halved glacé cherry.

5 Bake for 10–15 minutes until risen and golden brown.

# Cookies

There's nothing like home made cookies – they're always wonderful.

**Makes 12**

50 g (1¾ oz) low fat spread
25 g (1 oz) caster sugar
75 g (2¾ oz) plain flour
¼ teaspoon vanilla or almond essence

---

**1** *ProPoints* value per serving
**15** *ProPoints* values per recipe

**44 calories** per serving

Takes **10 minutes** to prepare + cooling,
**20 minutes** to bake

V

✳ not recommended

1 Preheat the oven to Gas Mark 4/180°C/fan oven 160°C.

2 Cream together the low fat spread and sugar. Stir in the flour and vanilla or almond essence to make a firm dough. (If you have the time, chill the dough for 30 minutes before continuing.)

3 Divide into 12 portions.

4 Take each portion, roll into a ball and then flatten and place on a non stick baking tray.

5 Bake for 15–20 minutes, until pale golden. Leave to cool on the baking tray for 5 minutes and then transfer to a cooling rack.

# Oat and Cherry Biscuits

Great little snacks that everyone will love.

**Makes 12 small biscuits**

50 g (1¾ oz) plain flour
½ teaspoon bicarbonate of soda
4 tablespoons artificial sweetener
100 g (3½ oz) porridge oats
50 g (1¾ oz) glacé cherries, chopped
75 g (2¾ oz) low fat spread

**2 ProPoints** values per serving
**26 ProPoints** values per recipe

**80 calories** per serving

Takes **20 minutes**

V

✱ not recommended

1 Preheat the oven to Gas Mark 3/160°C/fan oven 140°C. Sift the flour and bicarbonate of soda into a bowl and then add the sweetener, oats and cherries.

2 Melt the low fat spread in a small saucepan over a low heat and pour this into the dry mixture. Mix together. Cover a baking tray with baking parchment. Take walnut sized amounts of the mixture in your hands, flatten slightly to make a small biscuit shape and place on the baking tray. Leave a little space between each biscuit to allow them to spread in the oven.

3 Bake for 10 minutes or until golden brown.

**Store cupboard** Keep some glacé cherries in a jar or plastic container in your store cupboard. You'll find them in the baking section of any supermarket.

# Cinnamon Cookies

These light cookies can be cut into shapes such as stars, hearts and moons and used for Christmas decorations.

**Makes 30 biscuits**

**250 g (9 oz) self raising flour**
**1 tablespoon ground cinnamon**
**1 tablespoon ground ginger**
**6 tablespoons artificial sweetener**
**75 g (2¾ oz) low fat spread**
**1 large egg white**
**2 tablespoons golden syrup or honey**
**1 tablespoon icing sugar, to dust**

**1** *ProPoints* value per serving
**36** *ProPoints* values per recipe

**46 calories** per servin3

Takes **20 minutes** to prepare +
**30 minutes** chilling + cooling,
**15 minutes** to bake

V

✳ recommended (uncooked dough)

1 Preheat the oven to Gas Mark 3/160°C/fan oven 140°C. Place the flour, cinnamon, ginger and sweetener in a large bowl and stir together. Add the low fat spread and rub into the mixture with your hands until it resembles fine breadcrumbs.

2 Beat the egg white and the syrup or honey together in a jug or small bowl. Make a well in the middle of the flour mixture and add the egg mix.

3 Mix everything together gently, until you have a ball of soft dough. Wrap in a plastic bag or baking parchment and refrigerate for 30 minutes or so as this will help when rolling it out.

4 Roll out the dough on a floured surface until about 5 mm (¼ inch) thick. Cut out approximately 25 biscuits using cutters about 5 cm (2 inches) in diameter. Line a baking tray with baking parchment.

5 Place the shapes on the baking tray and bake for 15 minutes, until golden brown. Place on a cooling rack to cool. Dust with icing sugar to serve.

**Tips** To measure tablespoons of golden syrup or honey, first dip the measuring spoon into boiling water so the syrup won't stick.

The cookies can be kept in an airtight tin for up to a week.

# Italian Buns

Try serving one of these Mediterranean style buns with a warming soup as a hearty lunchtime filler.

Makes 8 buns

**450 g (1 lb) strong white flour, plus
1 tablespoon extra for kneading**
**1 teaspoon salt**
**1 sachet easy blend yeast**
**1 teaspoon caster sugar**
**15 g (½ oz) torn fresh basil**
**25 g (1 oz) stoned green or black olives,
diced**
**1 tablespoon extra virgin olive oil**
**freshly ground mixed pepper**

---

**6 *ProPoints*** values per serving
**52 *ProPoints*** values per recipe

**215 calories** per serving

Takes **25 minutes** to prepare +
**1½ hours** rising, **20 minutes** to bake

V

✳ recommended

1 Sift the flour into a warmed mixing bowl. Stir in the salt, yeast, sugar, basil and olives.

2 Add 300 ml (10 fl oz) of hand hot water and, using clean hands, bring the mixture together to form a dough ball. Knead the dough on a lightly floured surface for 5 minutes.

3 Place the dough in a clean bowl, cover with a damp tea towel and leave it to rise for 1 hour.

4 Turn the dough out on to a clean surface and knead again for 2 minutes. Shape the dough into eight balls. Arrange them on a non stick baking tray and cover them with a damp tea towel. Leave to rise in a warm place for about 30 minutes.

5 Preheat the oven to Gas Mark 6/200°C/fan oven 180°C. Brush the tops of the buns with olive oil and sprinkle the surface with a little freshly ground mixed pepper.

6 Bake the buns for 15–20 minutes until the bases sound hollow when tapped.

**Tip** The secret of cooking with yeast is to keep everything warm. This allows the yeast to react and rise well. An airing cupboard is a good place to allow the dough to rise. Cold temperatures can slow down the process considerably.

# Banana and Fig Loaf

A lovely moist fruit loaf for those who like figs.

**Serves 10**

150 g (5½ oz) All Bran
200 ml (7 fl oz) skimmed milk
100 g (3½ oz) fructose
1 egg, beaten
100 g (3½ oz) no soak dried figs, chopped
2 small bananas, mashed
1 teaspoon ground nutmeg
50 g (1¾ oz) sultanas
175 g (6 oz) self raising flour

**5 *ProPoints*** values per serving
**53 *ProPoints*** values per recipe

**200 calories** per serving

Takes **15 minutes** to prepare
+ **20 minutes** soaking + **20 minutes**
cooling, **1 hour** to bake.

V

✳ not recommended

1 Place the All Bran in a bowl and pour over the milk. Stir well and leave to stand for 20 minutes.

2 Preheat the oven to Gas Mark 4/180°C/fan oven 160°C. Line a 450 g (1 lb) loaf tin with non stick baking parchment.

3 Stir the fructose, egg, figs, bananas, nutmeg, sultanas and flour into the All Bran and milk mixture.

4 Spoon into the prepared tin, level the top with the back of a spoon and bake for 1 hour until firm to the touch. Leave to cool in the tin for 20 minutes and then transfer to a wire rack. Allow the loaf to cool completely before cutting into slices to serve.

# Cinnamon Prune Buns

These sweet and sticky rolls are based on Chelsea buns, with a filling of moist prunes and cinnamon sugar.

**Makes 12**

350 g (12 oz) plain flour, plus 1 tablespoon for kneading and rolling
½ teaspoon salt
7 g sachet active dried yeast
30 g (1¼ oz) low fat spread
1 egg, beaten
150 ml (5 fl oz) skimmed milk, warmed to body temperature
2 teaspoons cinnamon
40 g (1½ oz) soft light brown sugar
200 g (7 oz) dried prunes, chopped
low fat cooking spray
1 tablespoon clear honey, warmed

---

**5 ProPoints** values per serving
**58 ProPoints** values per recipe

C **168 calories** per serving

Takes **25 minutes** to prepare + **1½ hours** rising + **30 minutes** to proving, **25 minutes** to bake

V

✳ recommended

1 Sift the flour and salt into a mixing bowl, stir in the yeast, then rub in half the low fat spread.

2 Make a well in the centre, then mix in the egg and enough warmed milk to make a soft, but not sticky, dough that comes away from the bowl.

3 Dust the work surface with a ½ tablespoon flour, turn the dough out and knead for 3–4 minutes until soft and springy.

4 Return the dough to a clean bowl, cover with cling film and leave to rise in a warm place for 1½ hours or until doubled in size.

5 Sprinkle the remaining flour on to the work surface and roll out the dough to a 25 x 35 cm (10 x 14 inch) rectangle.

6 Melt the remaining low fat spread and brush all over the dough.

7 Mix the cinnamon and sugar together and sprinkle on evenly. Scatter the prunes on top and press in lightly.

8 Starting from one of the long sides, roll up the dough tightly, then slice into 12 pieces. Transfer to a roasting tin, lightly sprayed with the cooking spray, which will hold the buns fairly snugly. Cover with cling film and leave to prove and swell for 30 minutes.

9 Preheat the oven to Gas Mark 4/180°C/fan oven 160°C.

10 Bake the buns for 20–25 minutes until puffy, golden and springy. Remove from the oven and brush with the warmed honey. Serve slightly warm.

# Golden Raspberry Buns

A sweet treat to round off a meal, these are a great addition to a packed lunch.

**Makes 8**

**2 eggs, separated**
**200 g (7 oz) low fat natural yogurt**
**150 g (5½ oz) apple sauce (see Tip)**
**100 g (3½ oz) instant dried polenta or cornmeal**
**3 tablespoons artificial sweetener**
**a pinch of salt**
**½ teaspoon cream of tartar**
**150 g (5½ oz) raspberries**
**low fat cooking spray**

**2 *ProPoints*** values per serving
**20 *ProPoints*** values per recipe

**101 calories** per serving

Takes **15 minutes** to prepare + cooling, **15–20 minutes** to bake

V

❋ recommended

1 Preheat the oven to Gas Mark 4/180°C/fan oven 160°C.

2 Mix the egg yolks with the yogurt and apple sauce, then stir in the polenta, sweetener and a pinch of salt.

3 In a separate bowl, whisk the egg whites and cream of tartar to the soft peak stage. Stir a spoonful into the batter to slacken the mixture, then carefully fold in the remainder. Stir in 100 g (3½ oz) of raspberries, then spoon the batter into a non stick bun tin, lightly sprayed with the cooking spray. Scatter the remaining raspberries on top of each bun.

4 Bake for 15–20 minutes until firm, then cool slightly on a wire rack before eating.

**Tip** To make apple sauce, put 3 peeled, cored and sliced cooking apples, 6 cloves and 1 tablespoon of cider vinegar in a saucepan with 3 tablespoons of water. Cover and cook over a medium heat for 5 minutes or until the apples break down. Stir the sauce until smooth and then add 1 tablespoon of artificial sweetener, if needed. Remove the cloves before using.

# Healthy Herb Bread

Sprinkling the surface of the loaves with a little cold water just before putting them into the oven will help them to rise.

Serves 30

**500 g (1 lb 2 oz) strong white bread flour**

**300 g (10½ oz) soft grain strong white flour**

**100 g (3½ oz) coarse wheat bran**

**50 g (1¾ oz) coarse rye flour**

**50 g (1¾ oz) coarse oatmeal**

**100 g (3½ oz) sunflower, pumpkin and linseeds, mixed**

**1 packet easy-blend yeast**

**1 tablespoon salt**

**15 g (½ oz) fresh mixed herbs (e.g. parsley, thyme, rosemary, marjoram, chives)**

**250 g (9 oz) low fat natural yogurt**

**1 tablespoon olive oil**

**low fat cooking spray**

**4 ProPoints** values per serving
**118 ProPoints** values per recipe

**135 calories** per serving

Takes **25 minutes** to prepare + **1 hour 40 minutes** rising time, **50 minutes** to cook

V

\* recommended

1 In a very large mixing bowl, combine all the dry ingredients.

2 In a large jug, mix together the yogurt and 850 ml (1½ pints) of lukewarm water. Add to the dry flour mixture and stir to combine, then transfer to a floured surface and knead for 10–15 minutes until the dough is smooth and elastic.

3 Put the dough into a clean bowl and smear the olive oil on top. Cover the bowl with cling film or a clean, damp tea towel and leave for about an hour in a draught free place, or until the dough has roughly doubled in size.

4 Knock back the dough by punching it with your fist and then knead lightly for a few moments. Divide into two equal pieces and form into two ovals. Place on to separate baking trays, sprayed with the cooking spray. Allow the dough to rise in a warm place for a further 30–40 minutes.

5 Preheat the oven to Gas Mark 5/190°C/fan oven 170°C.

6 Bake for 40–50 minutes, or until the loaves are well risen and golden brown. They should have a hollow sound when tapped lightly on the bases.

**Tip** Seeds, such as sunflower or pumpkin, as used in this recipe, are great for adding flavour and texture to bakes.

# Potato and Spring Onion Bread

Serve a chunk of this tempting soda bread with a bowl of soup or stew. Soda bread is best eaten on the day it is made, but it can also be frozen successfully.

**Serves 6**

**175 g (6 oz) self raising flour**
**½ teaspoon bicarbonate of soda**
**a pinch of salt**
**200 g (7 oz) potato, peeled and grated coarsely**
**6 spring onions, sliced**
**3 teaspoons freshly chopped thyme**
**1 egg**
**2 tablespoons skimmed milk**
**low fat cooking spray**
**freshly ground black pepper**

**4 *ProPoints*** values per serving
**22 *ProPoints*** values per recipe

**143 calories** per serving

Takes **10 minutes** to prepare + cooling, **40 minutes** to bake.

V

✳ recommended

1 Preheat the oven to Gas Mark 5/190°C/fan oven 170°C.

2 Sift the flour, bicarbonate of soda and a pinch of salt into a mixing bowl and season with pepper. Stir the grated potato, spring onions and 2 teaspoons of thyme into the flour until evenly mixed.

3 Beat the egg with the milk and mix in to form a soft, but not sticky, dough. Shape into a 15 cm (6 inch) round on a baking tray, lightly sprayed with the cooking spray, then mark into six wedges with a knife, but don't cut all the way through to the tray.

4 Scatter the remaining thyme over the loaf, then bake in the oven for 40 minutes, or until the loaf is really crisp and sounds hollow when the base is tapped. Cool slightly on a wire rack before eating.

**Cooking basics** To knead dough: on a smooth surface, turn out the dough and then fold it towards you. Quickly push down with the heel of your hand. Turn the dough and stretch it out. Repeat until the dough is firm and smooth. This will give it elasticity, allowing it to rise more easily.

# Mediterranean Bread

This soft bread can be served with salad and cheese or as a sweet topped with fruit, yogurt and honey, adding the extra *ProPoints* values as necessary.

Serves 4

**2 teaspoons dried yeast**
**1 teaspoon sugar**
**low fat cooking spray**
**2 x 145 g packets instant pizza mix**
**1 teaspoon oil, for greasing**
**2 or 3 fresh rosemary sprigs**
**sea salt**

7 *ProPoints* values per serving
26 *ProPoints* values per recipe

**240 calories** per serving

Takes **15 minutes** to prepare + **30 minutes** rising, **10–15 minutes** to bake

V

\*  not recommended

1  In a small mixing bowl, combine 225 ml (8 fl oz) of warm water, the yeast and sugar and leave for 15 minutes until frothy. Spray a 28 x 18 cm (11 x 7 inch) shallow baking tin with the cooking spray.

2  Meanwhile, put the pizza mix into a large bowl and make a well in the centre. Add the frothed yeast and mix to a soft dough. Turn out on to a floured surface and knead for 2–3 minutes until smooth in texture.

3  Press into the prepared baking tin, pushing the dough into the corners. Cover with cling film, greased with the teaspoon of oil, and leave to rise in a warm place for about 30 minutes or until doubled in height.

4  Meanwhile, preheat the oven to Gas Mark 7/220°C/fan oven 200°C. Make dimples all over the surface of the risen dough with your fingers and sprinkle with the rosemary and sea salt.

5  Bake for 10–15 minutes until golden.

**Variation** To make a sweet version, add 1 tablespoon of sugar to the dry pizza mix before adding the yeast. Sprinkle a little demerara sugar over the finished dough in the tin instead of the rosemary and salt. The *ProPoints* values will remain the same.

# Quick and Easy Wholemeal Bread

5 ProPoints value

Home made bread has many advantages over shop bought equivalents, including being less expensive and containing fewer additives. It is tasty, satisfying and you know how many *ProPoints* values are in it.

**Makes 2 medium loaves (16 slices each loaf)**

**900 g (2 lb) plain wholemeal flour, plus extra for sprinkling**
**10 g (¼ oz) salt**
**15 g (½ oz) soft brown sugar**
**15 g (½ oz) fresh yeast or 10 g (¼ oz) dried yeast**
**600 ml (20 fl oz) warm water**
**low fat cooking spray**

**5 *ProPoints*** values per serving
**83 *ProPoints*** values per loaf

**95 calories** per serving

Takes **15 minutes** to prepare + **45–60 minutes** rising, **40** minutes to bake

V

✻ recommended

1 Stir the flour, salt and sugar together in a large bowl. Make a well in the centre.

2 Mix the yeast into a wet paste with a little warm water and pour into the well with a little more of the water.

3 Mix together with your hands, adding more water if it is too dry, until you have a slippery dough that comes away from the bowl in a smooth ball. Different flours vary in their absorbency so add the water a bit at a time in case the dough becomes too wet and sticky.

4 Divide the dough between two 23 x 13 cm (9 x 5 inch) bread tins which have been warmed and sprayed with the cooking spray. Cover with a clean, damp tea towel and leave in a warm place until the dough has risen by more than a half, usually around 45–60 minutes.

5 Preheat the oven to Gas Mark 6/200°C/fan oven 180°C. Sprinkle the loaves with flour and bake for 35–40 minutes. Check that they are cooked by tapping the bottom – they should sound hollow.

**Tip** This recipe makes two medium loaves – one to eat and one to wrap in a plastic bag and freeze for up to 3 months. Uncooked bread will rise if you leave it in the fridge, but it will take 24 hours. It's not absolutely necessary to put it in a warm place, although this does speed up the process. If you put it in an airing cupboard or on top of the oven, the dough will rise quickly, giving a more open texture than if left in the kitchen for 1½ hours, when it rises very gently.

# Easy Rosemary Beer Bread

**4** ProPoints value

This clever recipe uses real ale to bind everything together, and it gives the bread a wonderful yeasty flavour.

Makes 10 slices

**350 g (12 oz) wholemeal flour**
**1 teaspoon baking powder**
**25 g (1 oz) sun-dried tomatoes, chopped finely**
**2 teaspoons finely chopped fresh rosemary**
**½ teaspoon salt**
**300 ml (10 fl oz) real ale**
**2 teaspoons olive oil**

**4** *ProPoints* values per serving
**38** *ProPoints* values per recipe

**120 calories** per serving

Takes **15 minutes** to prepare,
**30 minutes** to bake

V

✳ recommended

1 Preheat the oven to Gas Mark 6/200°C/fan oven 180°C. Line a 700 g (1 lb 9 oz) loaf tin with non stick baking parchment.

2 Place the wholemeal flour in a bowl and stir in the baking powder, chopped sun-dried tomatoes, rosemary and salt.

3 Make a well in the centre of the dry ingredients. Add the ale and olive oil and mix to a firm dough. Press the dough into the loaf tin and score the top. Bake for 30 minutes, until well risen and the base of the bread sounds hollow when tapped.

**Tip** If you can, use good quality extra virgin olive oil; it can be expensive but makes all the difference. Try other flavours instead of the tomatoes, such as a teaspoon of wholegrain mustard or 25 g (1 oz) of sliced, stoned black olives, but remember to amend the *ProPoints* values accordingly.

# Pies, Tarts and Pastries

There are few things more satisfying than producing a beautiful fruit tart or pie to round off a perfect meal. We've included a classic French Apple Tart, as well as more unusual combinations such as Rhubarb Lasagne, Lime Cheesecake Tarts and Nectarine and Strawberry Tart. The mouth watering recipes in this section will inspire you to get out your rolling pin and be creative with pastry.

Pastry and fruit are the perfect partners, but pasta can make a wonderful fruit pie too

# Nectarine and Strawberry Tart

This looks like a long recipe, but it's very straightforward. All you need is patience when making the custard and arranging the fruit. It's well worth it.

**Serves 6**

1½ tablespoons plain flour
125 g (4½ oz) ready made shortcrust pastry
1 egg yolk, beaten
25 g (1 oz) caster sugar
½ teaspoon vanilla essence
150 ml (5 fl oz) skimmed milk
2 heaped teaspoons reduced sugar
   apricot jam
½ teaspoon lemon juice
150 g (5½ oz) small strawberries, halved
1 nectarine, halved, stone removed and then
   sliced thinly into half moon shapes

---

**4 ProPoints** values per serving
**26 ProPoints** values per recipe

**181 calories** per serving

Takes **45 minutes** + cooling

V

* not recommended

1 Preheat the oven to Gas Mark 6/200°C/fan oven 180°C.

2 Lightly dust a work surface with half a tablespoon of the flour and roll out the pastry to make a 24 cm (9½ inch) circle. Use this to line a 20 cm (8 inch) non stick flan tin. Prick the base all over with a fork and line with foil or baking parchment. Fill with baking beans.

3 Bake the pastry case for 12 minutes, then remove the foil or baking parchment and beans and bake for a further 7–8 minutes, or until the pastry is an even golden brown. Leave to cool in the tin.

4 Meanwhile, make the custard. Use an electric beater to whisk the egg yolk and sugar together until it thickens and changes to a light cream colour. Stir in the remaining flour and vanilla and gradually whisk in the milk. Transfer to a small non stick saucepan on a low heat and stir continuously until the mixture comes to a simmer and starts to thicken. This could take 10 minutes or so. Keep stirring for 2 minutes then remove from the heat and leave to cool completely.

5 In a small bowl, mix the apricot jam with the lemon juice and half a teaspoon of water.

6 When everything is cold, carefully transfer the pastry case to the serving plate and brush the inside with half of the apricot jam mix. Spread the custard over the jam – don't worry if it's not even; it will be hidden under the fruit. Arrange the fruit on top of the custard. Start with three halved strawberries in the centre then fan out the nectarine slices in a circle around it. Once you have the basic shape, slide extra nectarine slices between the others until they're all used up. Finish with strawberry halves around the edge.

7 Heat the remaining apricot jam mix in a microwave for a few seconds to thin it a little, then brush it over the fruit to glaze. If you don't have a microwave, stand it in boiling water for a few minutes. Chill the tart until required and use a sharp knife to cut it into six slices to serve.

# Eccles Swirls

Easy and fun to make, these filo pastry swirls will melt in the mouth. Work quickly with filo pastry as, once unrolled, it becomes dry and brittle after a short time.

**Serves 10**

**100 g (3½ oz) currants**
**25 g (1 oz) caster sugar**
**1 teaspoon ground nutmeg**
**½ teaspoon ground cinnamon**
**25 g (1 oz) mixed peel**
**1 cooking apple, peeled, cored and grated**
**6 x 15 g filo pastry sheets**
**low fat cooking spray**
**1 tablespoon demerara sugar**

---

2 *ProPoints* values per serving
21 *ProPoints* values per recipe

C    **133 calories** per serving

Takes **15 minutes** to prepare,
**15 minutes** to bake

V

✳   recommended

1 Preheat the oven to Gas Mark 5/190°C/fan oven 170°C.

2 Mix together the currants, caster sugar, nutmeg, cinnamon, mixed peel and grated apple.

3 Spray the filo sheets with the cooking spray. Stack two sheets together and sprinkle with a third of the currant mixture. Top with another two sheets sprayed with the cooking spray and then another third of the currant mixture. Finally, top with the two remaining filo pastry sheets and the last of the currant mixture. Roll up like a Swiss roll and then slice at 2.5 cm (1 inch) intervals. Lift on to a non stick baking tray and sprinkle with demerara sugar.

4 Bake for 12–15 minutes, until golden and crisp.

**Cooking basics** If using frozen filo pastry, allow it to thaw in the pack and then take out the sheets and stack them on a clean, slightly damp cloth. While you work, cover the sheets with the damp cloth and use the sheets one at a time, making sure you spray them with cooking spray. Covering the pastry in this way will help to keep it moist as it dries out very quickly when it's exposed to air.

# Apple and Walnut Pie

Hurrah for filo pastry. Low in fat and easy to use, it means that we can enjoy countless favourite pies and flans, without using too many *ProPoints* values.

**Serves 8**

25 g (1 oz) walnut pieces, toasted
25 g (1 oz) low fat spread
50 g (1¾ oz) caster sugar
1 egg
grated zest and juice of a small lemon
25 g (1 oz) self raising flour
1 teaspoon ground cinnamon
8 crisp eating apples (e.g. Cox's)
270 g packet filo pastry sheets
low fat cooking spray
icing sugar, for dusting

---

**4 *ProPoints*** values per serving
**34 *ProPoints*** values per recipe

C  **222 calories** per serving

Takes **15 minutes** to prepare,
**45 minutes** to bake

V

✱  recommended

1 Preheat the oven to Gas Mark 5/190°C/fan oven 170°C. Whizz the walnuts in a food processor until finely chopped. In a small bowl, cream together the low fat spread and 40 g (1½ oz) of sugar. Whisk in the egg and then the lemon zest, flour and ½ teaspoon of cinnamon. Finally mix in the walnuts.

2 Peel and slice the apples and toss with the remaining sugar, cinnamon and lemon juice.

3 Line a 23 cm (9 inch) flan tin with three quarters of the filo pastry, allowing the edges to overhang. Spread the walnut paste over the base and top with the apples. Gather up the overhanging pastry, scrunching the sheets up like paper. Scrunch up the remaining pastry and use to completely conceal the apple filling.

4 Spray the top lightly with the cooking spray and bake for 40–45 minutes. Cover lightly with foil if the pastry browns too much.

5 Serve warm, dusted with some sieved icing sugar.

# Yorkshire Curd Tarts

These melt in the mouth treats are rather like mini cheesecakes, but are much lower in *ProPoints* values.

**Makes 12 tarts**

175 g (6 oz) ready made shortcrust pastry,
  defrosted if frozen
125 g (4½ oz) low fat cottage cheese
finely grated zest of a lemon
25 g (1 oz) sultanas
25 g (1 oz) demerara sugar
a pinch of ground nutmeg
1 egg

3 *ProPoints* values per serving
31 *ProPoints* values per recipe

C  115 calories per serving

Takes **20 minutes** to prepare,
**20 minutes** to bake

V

✱  recommended

1 Preheat the oven to Gas Mark 5/190°C/fan oven 170°C. Roll out the pastry and cut out circles. Fit them in a 12 hole patty tin.

2 Push the cottage cheese through a sieve and beat it well with the lemon zest, sultanas, sugar, nutmeg and egg.

3 Divide the filling between the pastry cases and bake for 20 minutes, until the filling is just set to the touch.

**Tip** For a change, try adding grated orange zest instead of lemon and ground cinnamon instead of the nutmeg. Dust 1 teaspoon of icing sugar over the total number of tarts, if desired, which will not alter the *ProPoints* values.

# American Apple Pie

The warm, spicy flavour of cinnamon gives this American apple pie its distinctive appeal.

**Serves 8**

**700 g (1 lb 9 oz) cooking apples, peeled, cored and sliced**
**2 tablespoons lemon juice**
**½ teaspoon ground cinnamon**
**75 g (2¾ oz) unrefined caster sugar**
**low fat cooking spray**
**8 x 15 g filo pastry sheets**
**2 teaspoons icing sugar, for dusting**
**8 tablespoons half fat crème fraîche, to serve**

1 Put the apples in a large saucepan with the lemon juice, cinnamon and sugar. Add 2 tablespoons of water, and then cover and simmer for 5–8 minutes, until they are tender. Remove from the heat and allow to cool completely.

2 Preheat the oven to Gas Mark 6/200°C/fan oven 180°C. Lightly spray a 23 cm (9 inch) pie dish with the cooking spray.

3 Line the pie dish with half the pastry sheets, spraying each sheet with the cooking spray and overlapping the edges of the tin slightly. Bake the pie in the centre of the oven for 4–5 minutes.

4 Spoon the cooled apples into the pastry case. Top with the remaining pastry sheets, spraying each sheet 2–3 times with the cooking spray. Make loose folds in the pastry so that it fits over the top of the pie dish and then trim off any excess. Spray the surface another 2–3 times with the cooking spray and bake in the oven for 15–20 minutes until golden.

5 Let the pie cool for a few minutes and then serve, dusted with the icing sugar and accompanied by the crème fraîche.

---

C **4 ProPoints** values per serving
**30 ProPoints** values per recipe

C **160 calories** per serving

⊘ Takes **20 minutes** to prepare + cooling,
**20 minutes** to bake

V

✳ recommended

**Variation** Use ground mixed spice instead of the cinnamon, if you prefer. The **ProPoints** values will remain the same.

# Fruity Filo Tarts

Try to use ripe pears for these fruity tarts, so that the juices run and start to caramelise as they cook.

**Serves 4**

**2 x 45 g frozen filo pastry sheets, defrosted**
**25 g (1 oz) low fat spread, melted**
**2 ripe pears, halved**
**2 teaspoons caster sugar**
**100 g (3½ oz) raspberries**

1 Preheat the oven to Gas Mark 6/200°C/fan oven 180°C.

2 Brush each sheet of filo lightly with the melted low fat spread. Fold in half lengthways, then into thirds, and cut each folded sheet into two rectangles.

3 Place on a baking tray and brush the top with melted low fat spread. Remove the cores from the pears using a teaspoon then slice and arrange on the pastry bases. Sprinkle with sugar and bake on a high shelf for 8 minutes.

4 Scatter the raspberries on top and bake for a further 4 minutes. Serve warm.

**2 ProPoints** values per serving
**10 ProPoints** values per recipe

C **136 calories** per serving

Takes **20 minutes**

V

✱ not recommended

**Tip** You can find frozen filo pastry packs that weigh 270 g for 6 sheets in major supermarkets. This will give you the size of sheet you need for this recipe.

# Pineapple Tarte Tatin

This simple yet effective dessert is a delicious variation on the classic tarte tatin.

**Serves 8**

**1 teaspoon plain white flour, for rolling**
**150 g (5½ oz) puff pastry**
**227 g can pineapple rings in natural juice, drained and halved**
**15 g (½ oz) low fat spread, melted**
**2 tablespoons demerara sugar**

---

© **3 ProPoints** values per serving
**22 ProPoints** values per recipe

C **98 calories** per serving

⊙ Takes **15 minutes** to prepare + **10 minutes** cooling, **25 minutes** to bake

**V**

✳ recommended

1 Preheat the oven to Gas Mark 5/190°C/fan oven 170°C.

2 Lightly dust a work surface with flour and roll out the puff pastry to make a 23 cm (9 inch) circle.

3 Arrange the pineapple rings in a 20 cm (8 inch) tarte tatin dish or a round cake tin. Drizzle the melted low fat spread over the pineapple and then sprinkle over the demerara sugar. Lay the pastry circle over the top of the fruit and tuck in the edges.

4 Bake the tart in the oven for 25 minutes. Allow it to cool for 10 minutes. Then place a plate on top and turn the dish or tin upside down so the tart drops on to the plate. Serve the tart warm or cold, sliced into wedges.

# Fresh Fig Tart

What better way to use a fresh fig and give yourself a delicious treat?

**Serves 1**

**low fat cooking spray**
**40 g (1½ oz) ready rolled puff pastry**
**1 fig, quartered**
**2 teaspoons honey**
**finely grated zest and juice of ½ an orange**

---

**7 *ProPoints* values per serving**
**7 *ProPoints* values per recipe**

C  **199 calories** per serving

Takes **20 minutes**

V

\*  not recommended

1 Preheat the oven to Gas Mark 7/220ºC/fan oven 200ºC. Spray a baking tray with the cooking spray.

2 Unwrap the pastry and trim the edges. Cut out a 12 x 12 cm (4½ x 4½ inch) square. The remaining pastry can be frozen.

3 Arrange the fig quarters on top of the pastry. Mix the honey with the orange zest and juice. Drizzle a teaspoon over the tart, reserving the rest.

4 Bake on the baking tray for 12–15 minutes until the pastry is puffed and golden. Serve warm with the reserved juice spooned over.

# Tiny Cheesecake Tarts

With the taste of traditional cheesecake, these bite size tarts are great for a party.

**Makes 12**

**150 g (5½ oz) sweet shortcrust pastry, thawed if frozen**

**100 g (3½ oz) cottage cheese**

**1 small egg, beaten**

**25 g (1 oz) currants**

**25 g (1 oz) golden caster sugar**

**finely grated zest of a lemon**

**a pinch of ground nutmeg**

1 Preheat the oven to Gas Mark 4/180°C/fan oven 160°C.

2 Roll out the pastry on a lightly floured surface. Use to line 12 small tartlet tins or a 12 hole patty tin, using a fork to prick the base of each one. Place the tins on a baking tray.

3 Mix together the cottage cheese, egg, currants and sugar. Spoon the mixture into the pastry lined patty tins. Sprinkle each one with lemon zest and ground nutmeg.

4 Bake for 20–25 minutes, until set and golden brown. Serve warm or cold.

2 *ProPoints* values per serving
28 *ProPoints* values per recipe

c  85 calories per serving

Takes **20 minutes** to prepare,
**25 minutes** to bake

V

✳  not recommended

# Rhubarb Lasagne

This ingenious sweet lasagne uses the classic combination of rhubarb and custard as a filling.

**Serves 4**

**500 g (1 lb 2 oz) fresh rhubarb, cut into 2.5 cm (1 inch) chunks**
**2 heaped tablespoons artificial sweetener**
**6 sheets (125 g/4½ oz) no precook lasagne**
**425 g can low fat custard**
**2 teaspoons flaked almonds**

1 Preheat the oven to Gas Mark 8/230°C/fan oven 210°C.

2 Put the rhubarb into a baking dish, sprinkle with 2 tablespoons of water, then bake for about 5–8 minutes until tender. Remove from the oven and sprinkle with the sweetener.

3 Reduce the oven temperature to Gas Mark 5/190°C/fan oven 170°C.

4 Spoon half the rhubarb into a 23 x 18 cm (9 x 7 inch) baking dish and top with two lasagne sheets. Cover with half the custard, spreading it over evenly. Add another two sheets of lasagne, then the remaining rhubarb. Top with the last two lasagne sheets and spread the remaining custard over. Sprinkle with flaked almonds.

5 Bake in the oven for 25–30 minutes then serve.

**6 *ProPoints*** values per serving
**26 *ProPoints*** values per recipe

C **215 calories** per serving

Takes **35 minutes** to prepare,
**30 minutes** to bake

V

* not recommended

# Lime Cheesecake Tarts

These light filo tarts have the zesty taste of lime. They taste great as well as look great.

**Makes 8**

**3 x 15 g filo pastry sheets, measuring
30 x 17 cm (12 x 7 inches)**
**low fat cooking spray**
**250 g tub Quark**
**finely grated zest and juice of a lime plus
extra zest, to decorate**
**75 g (2¾ oz) caster sugar**

2 *ProPoints* values per serving
16 *ProPoints* values per recipe

111 **calories** per serving

20 **minutes** to prepare + cooling,
10 **minutes** to bake

✱ not recommended

1 Preheat the oven to Gas Mark 4/180ºC/fan oven 160ºC.

2 Cut each filo sheet into eight squares. Using a 12 hole bun tin, place a square of filo in the middle of a hole, spray with the cooking spray and then layer a further two sheets on top, spraying each one as you go. Layer each one diagonally so that you end up with a 12 pointed star that creates a basket. Repeat with the remaining pastry sheets to make eight baskets. Bake for 10 minutes until golden and crisp. Cool in the tin.

3 Beat together the Quark, lime zest, lime juice and sugar until smooth.

4 Add the Quark mixture to the baskets and serve decorated with a little lime zest.

# Strawberry and Apple Filo Tart

This delicious tart is perfect for dinner parties.

**Serves 6**

**low fat cooking spray**
**150 g (5½ oz) filo pastry**
**3 eating apples**
**50 ml (2 fl oz) fresh orange juice**
**2 tablespoons artificial sweetener**
**300 g (10½ oz) strawberries, hulled and halved**

**To serve**

**2 teaspoons icing sugar**
**6 tablespoons half fat crème fraîche**

---

**4 _ProPoints_** values per serving
**21 _ProPoints_** values per recipe

**C**   **155 calories** per serving

Takes **20 minutes** to prepare,
**30 minutes** to bake

**V**

✻   not recommended

1 Preheat the oven to Gas Mark 6/200°C/fan oven 180°C. Spray the base of a 23 cm (9 inch) flan tin with the cooking spray.

2 Line the flan tin with half the pastry sheets, spraying each sheet with the cooking spray and overlapping the edges of the tin slightly.

3 Bake for 10 minutes in the centre of the oven.

4 Meanwhile, peel, core and slice the apples, then put them in a saucepan with the orange juice. Cover and simmer for about 5–8 minutes, until tender. Remove from the heat and add the sweetener and strawberries, mixing gently. Use to fill the cooked flan case.

5 Tear the remaining pastry sheets into strips and arrange them loosely over the tart. Spray two or three times with the cooking spray, then bake for a further 15–20 minutes.

6 Cool the tart for a few minutes, then serve, dusted with icing sugar and accompanied by the crème fraîche.

**Tip** You can use sunflower low fat cooking spray instead of the olive oil variety; its flavour is more suitable.

# Plum Pie

This delicious pie has a sweet, wholemeal pastry base, topped with plums in a cheesecake batter mix.

**Serves 6**

**low fat cooking spray**

**For the base**
**75 g (2¾ oz) low fat spread**
**50 g (1¾ oz) caster sugar**
**50 g (1¾ oz) self raising flour**
**50 g (1¾ oz) wholemeal self raising flour**
**1 egg**

**For the filling**
**570 g can plums in natural juice, drained**
**150 ml (5 fl oz) low fat natural yogurt**
**1 egg**
**½ teaspoon vanilla essence**
**40 g (1½ oz) caster sugar**

1 Preheat the oven to Gas Mark 6/200°C/fan oven 180°C and spray an 18 cm (7 inch) tin with the cooking spray.

2 Place all the base ingredients in a food processor and process until blended. If you do not have a food processor then cream the low fat spread and caster sugar together, mix in the flours then the egg.

3 Spoon the mixture into the prepared tin and smooth down with the back of a spoon. Stone and halve the plums and arrange over the top of the base.

4 Beat together all the other filling ingredients. Pour over the plums and bake for 30 minutes or until the edges are a deep golden brown and the filling is just set (it becomes firmer as the pie cools). Transfer to a wire rack and cut into triangles. Best served warm.

5 *ProPoints* values per serving
32 *ProPoints* values per recipe

C   **238 calories** per serving

Takes **15 minutes** to prepare,
**30 minutes** to bake

V

*   recommended

**Variation** Use eight fresh plums instead of canned plums, for the same *ProPoints* values per serving.

# Deluxe Mince Parcels

These little filo parcels are a delicious festive treat.

**Makes 12 parcels**

**125 g (4½ oz) mincemeat**
**2 small ripe bananas, diced finely**
**1 dessert apple, peeled,**
  **cored and grated**

**6 x 15 g filo pastry sheets,**
  **measuring 30 x 18 cm**
  **(12 x 7 inches)**
**1 egg, beaten**
**2 teaspoons icing sugar, to dust**

1 Preheat the oven to Gas Mark 6/200°C/fan oven 180°C.

2 In a mixing bowl, combine the mincemeat and fruit then set aside.

3 Lay a sheet of filo pastry on a clean, dry work surface. Cut it into two squares, then cut each of these into three rectangular strips.

4 Place three strips randomly on top of each other so that the corners point in different directions. Brush the edges with egg then place a spoonful of the mincemeat mixture in the centre. Scrunch the edges together to form a ruffle and place the parcel in a hole of a non stick bun tin, or on a non stick baking tray.

5 Repeat the process with the remaining pastry and mincemeat, then gently brush the parcels with the remaining egg. Bake them for 6–10 minutes until golden. Serve warm, dusted with icing sugar.

**2 ProPoints** values per serving
**19 ProPoints** values per recipe

C  **121 calories** per serving

Takes **25 minutes** to prepare,
**10 minutes** to bake

V

✻  not recommended

# Pecan Treacle Tart

This is a lusciously sweet and sticky pudding. Serve warm with a 60 g (2 oz) scoop of low fat vanilla ice cream, for an extra 2 *ProPoints* values per serving.

**Serves 6**

100 g (3½ oz) plain flour, plus 1 teaspoon for rolling
50 g (1¾ oz) low fat spread
200 g (7 oz) golden syrup
zest and juice of ½ a lemon
40 g (1½ oz) fresh breadcrumbs
25 g (1 oz) pecans, chopped
1 egg, beaten

© **7 *ProPoints*** values per serving
**42 *ProPoints*** values per recipe

C **250 calories** per serving

⊘ Takes **20 minutes** to prepare + **30 minutes** chilling + **15 minutes** cooling, **25 minutes** to bake

V

✳ not recommended

1 Sift the flour into a bowl and rub in the low fat spread until the mixture is crumbly. Mix in just enough cold water to bring the pastry together in a ball. Flatten into a disc, wrap in cling film and chill for 30 minutes.

2 Preheat the oven to Gas Mark 5/190°C/fan oven 170°C.

3 Warm the golden syrup with the lemon zest and juice until just runny. Stir in the breadcrumbs and leave to swell for 5 minutes.

4 Dust the work surface with 1 teaspoon of flour and roll out the pastry to fit a 24 cm (9½ inch) metal pie plate (or a disposable foil pie plate if you don't have a metal one).

5 Mix the pecans and beaten egg into the syrupy breadcrumbs, then pour the filling into the pastry case, place on a baking tray and bake for 25 minutes until the filling is set. Let the tart cool for at least 15 minutes before eating, as the filling will be very hot.

# French Apple Tarts

These delicious individual little tarts can be served hot or cold with 1 tablespoon low fat fromage frais per person, for an additional 1 *ProPoints* value per person – and they're great for a dinner party.

**Serves 6**

**low fat cooking spray**
**200 g (7 oz) ready rolled puff pastry**
**1 teaspoon icing sugar**
**½ teaspoon ground cinnamon**
**½ teaspoon ground cloves**
**2 dessert apples (e.g. Pink Lady, Fuji or Braeburn)**
**juice of ½ a lemon**

---

4 *ProPoints* values per serving
23 *ProPoints* values per recipe

C   **160 calories** per serving

Takes **15 minutes** to prepare, **15 minutes** to bake

V

✳   not recommended

1 Preheat the oven to Gas Mark 6/200°C/fan oven 180°C and spray a baking tray with the cooking spray.

2 Roll the pastry out further until it is about 5 mm (¼ inch) thick and then cut it into six squares and lay them on the prepared baking tray. With the tip of a sharp knife, score a border, about 2 cm (¾ inch) wide, around each.

3 Mix the icing sugar, cinnamon and cloves in a small bowl and place in a small sieve such as a tea strainer.

4 Core and slice the apples into thin slices and then toss them with the lemon juice in a bowl. Arrange the apple slices so that they overlap and cover the bases of the pastry squares, leaving the border of pastry around each one.

5 Dust each tart with the spice sugar and bake for 10–15 minutes, or until the pastry is golden brown and risen.

# Pear and Almond Tart

A light and scrumptious version of a classic French tart.

**Serves 6**

**For the pastry**

50 g (1¾ oz) low fat spread
100 g (3½ oz) plain flour
a pinch of salt

**For the filling**

410 g can pears in natural juice, drained,
    with 2 tablespoons of the juice reserved
2 eggs, beaten
175 ml (6 fl oz) low fat natural yogurt
½ teaspoon almond essence
50 g (1¾ oz) ground almonds
1 tablespoon reduced sugar jam, melted with
    1 tablespoon water

---

5 *ProPoints* values per serving
30 *ProPoints* values per recipe

C   **208 calories** per serving

Takes **40 minutes** to prepare
+ **30 minutes** chilling, **30 minutes** to bake

V

✱   recommended

1 Make the pastry by rubbing the low fat spread into the flour and salt until the mixture resembles fresh breadcrumbs, then add about 1 tablespoon of water and bring together quickly with your hand into a ball. Wrap the pastry in cling film and chill for 30 minutes.

2 Preheat the oven to Gas Mark 6/200°C/fan oven 180°C. Roll out the pastry in a circle about 5 mm (½ inch) thick and use to line a 19 cm (7½ inch) loose bottomed flan tin. Line with foil or baking parchment and fill with baking beans.

3 Bake blind for 15 minutes then remove the beans and lining and bake for a further 10 minutes or until evenly golden brown.

4 Arrange the pear halves cut side down in the pastry case. Beat together the eggs, yogurt, almond essence, almonds and pear juice. Pour around the pears. Brush the bits of pear still showing with the melted jam and bake for 30 minutes or until the top is firm and golden brown.

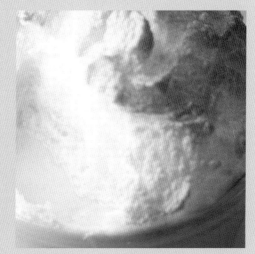

# Baked Desserts and Puddings

Few of us can resist a good pudding, and there is something special about a baked dessert that makes an occasion of any meal. In this chapter you'll find many traditional recipes, but often with a modern twist. Why not try Banana and Peach Crumble, Blueberry Baked Cheesecake, Summer Fruit Profiteroles and, everyone's favourite, Hot Chocolate Puds.

Hot puds look impressive and taste absolutely delicious

# Chocolate Roulade with Raspberry Crush

This is a quick and impressive dessert – it's great if friends drop round for supper.

**Serves 4**

**2 large eggs**
**80 g (3 oz) caster sugar**
**75 g (2¾ oz) plain white flour**
**2 tablespoons cocoa powder**
**a good pinch of salt**
**200 g (7 oz) fresh raspberries**
**200 g (7 oz) Quark**
**1 tablespoon clear honey (optional)**
**1 teaspoon of icing sugar, for dusting**

---

7 *ProPoints* values per serving
30 *ProPoints* values per recipe

**C** 285 calories per serving

Takes **20 minutes** + **5 minutes** cooling

**V**

✳ not recommended

1 Heat the oven to Gas Mark 6/200°C/fan oven 180°C. Line a Swiss roll tin, about 30 x 23 cm (12 x 9 inches), with non stick baking parchment.

2 Put the eggs and sugar in a large heatproof bowl, and place the bowl over a saucepan of simmering water. Using a hand held electric whisk (see Tip), beat the mixture steadily until you have a thick yellow foam – it should leave a trail when you lift out the whisk. Remove the bowl from the pan and let it cool.

3 Sift together the flour, cocoa powder and salt. Gently fold these dry ingredients into the eggy foam. Now spread the mixture into the prepared tin.

4 Bake in the oven for 8–10 minutes until the sponge is firm to the touch. Remove the tin from the oven and let it cool for 5 minutes. Turn the sponge out on to a wire rack and carefully peel off the lining paper. Trim off the crusty edges of the sponge and cover it with a fresh sheet of non stick baking parchment. Roll up the sponge, enclosing the parchment, and allow it to cool.

5 Meanwhile, place the raspberries in a bowl and crush them with a fork. Stir in the Quark. Sweeten the mixture with the honey, if using.

6 Unroll the sponge and remove the baking parchment. Spread it with the raspberry cream and then re-roll it. Place the roulade on a platter and sift over the icing sugar.

**Tip** Electric whisks are best for whisking eggs to a thick foam. Alternatively, if you have an electric mixer with a whisk attachment, then you can use that without having to beat the egg over a pan of simmering water.

# Apple Strudel

This traditional dessert from Austria and Germany is made with paper thin pastry, filled with spiced fruit.

**Serves 8**

**low fat cooking spray**
**finely grated zest and juice of a lemon**
**450 g (1 lb) cooking apples**
**40 g (1½ oz) light muscovado sugar**
**25 g (1 oz) fresh white breadcrumbs**
**25 g (1 oz) sultanas**
**1 teaspoon ground mixed spice**
**6 x 15 g filo pastry sheets, defrosted if frozen**
**2 teaspoons icing sugar, for dusting**

1 Preheat the oven to Gas Mark 5/190°C/fan oven 170°C. Spray a non stick baking tray with the cooking spray.

2 Put the lemon zest and juice into a large bowl. Peel, core and thinly slice the apples, adding them to the lemon juice as you go to prevent them from turning brown. Mix the sugar, breadcrumbs, sultanas and mixed spice into the apples.

3 Take two sheets of filo pastry and lay them side by side, long sides together. Overlap them by 5 cm (2 inches) and then spray once or twice with the cooking spray. Cover with two more sheets, overlapping and spraying as before, and then repeat until all six sheets of pastry have been used.

4 Spread the fruit mixture along one long edge of the pastry, fold in the two short sides, and then roll up carefully from the long edge to enclose the fruit. Place it on the prepared baking tray, curling the strudel to fit, if necessary.

5 Bake for 35–40 minutes, or until the apples are tender and the strudel is golden brown. Cool slightly, dust with the icing sugar and serve.

C. **2 ProPoints** values per serving
**16 ProPoints** values per recipe

C **100 calories** per serving

⌚ Takes **20 minutes** to prepare,
**40 minutes** to bake

V

✻ recommended

**Serving suggestion** Serve the strudel with 1 tablespoon of low fat natural yogurt, adding an extra 1 **ProPoints** value per serving.

# Baked Banana with Passion Fruit

A delicious baked dessert in minutes. The passion fruit adds an exotic fragrance to the fruit parcels.

**Serves 1**

**1 orange, peeled and sliced**
**1 banana, peeled and sliced thickly**
**1 passion fruit**
**1 tablespoon very low fat plain fromage frais**

1  Preheat the oven to Gas Mark 6/200°C/fan oven 180°C.

2  Place a large square of foil on a baking tray. Sit the orange slices in the centre, add the banana then scoop the seeds from the passion fruit and place on the banana.

3  Seal the parcel tightly, crimping and sealing the foil so that the juices can't escape. Bake for 7 minutes, then open up carefully and serve topped with the fromage frais.

**1 ProPoints** values per serving
**1 ProPoints** values per recipe

C  **188 calories** per serving

Takes **10 minutes**

V

✱  not recommended

# Lemon, Almond and Strawberry Gâteau

Decorate this light and lemony gâteau with strawberries, icing sugar and flower petals for a summery dinner party centrepiece.

**Serves 8**

**low fat cooking spray**
**6 eggs**
**6½ tablespoons artificial sweetener**
**finely grated zest and juice of a lemon**
**60 g (2 oz) ground almonds**
**50 g (1¾ oz) plain flour**
**2 drops almond essence**
**150 g (5½ oz) virtually fat free fromage frais**
**450 g (1 lb) strawberries, hulled and sliced**
**fresh mint, to decorate (optional)**

**4 ProPoints** values per serving
**28 ProPoints** values per recipe

**170 calories** per serving

Takes **15 minutes** to prepare + cooling, **45 minutes** to bake

V

＊  not recommended

1  Preheat the oven to Gas Mark 4/180°C/fan oven 160°C. Spray a 20 cm (8 inch) cake tin with the cooking spray and line it with non stick baking parchment.

2  Whisk the eggs until very pale and fluffy – this takes about 5 minutes of continuous whisking. Gently fold in 6 tablespoons of sweetener, the lemon zest and juice, ground almonds, flour and almond essence.

3  Pour the mixture into the tin. Bake for 45 minutes, until firm to the touch and coming away from the edges of the tin slightly.

4  Leave to cool in the tin for a few minutes. It will sink in the middle. Turn it out carefully and turn it over so that the golden top is uppermost.

5  Leave to cool for 1 hour. When cool, fold the remaining sweetener into the fromage frais and pile this on top of the cake. Top with the strawberries then decorate with fresh mint, if using.

# Baked Lemon Pudding

This pudding takes very little time to prepare and comes out of the oven ready to eat straightaway.

**Serves 4**

**40 g (1½ oz) low fat spread**
**80 g (3 oz) light soft brown sugar**
**grated zest and juice of a lemon**
**2 eggs, separated**
**80 g (3 oz) self raising flour, sifted**
**250 ml (9 fl oz) skimmed milk**

---

7 *ProPoints* values per serving
26 *ProPoints* values per recipe

C   **245 calories** per serving

Takes **10 minutes** to prepare,
**30 minutes** to bake

V

\*   not recommended

1 Preheat the oven to Gas Mark 6/200°C/fan oven 180°C.

2 Cream together the low fat spread, sugar and lemon zest.

3 Beat the egg yolks and add them, together with the flour, to the low fat spread mixture. Stir well.

4 Add the milk and the juice of the lemon. Keep stirring until you have a smooth batter.

5 Whisk the egg whites stiffly and then very gently fold into the mixture.

6 Pour into a 1.2 litre (2 pint) pie dish and place this in a roasting tin with 3 cm (1¼ inches) of water in the bottom.

7 Bake for 30 minutes, until firm and springy to the touch.

**Save time** You can buy a bottle of lemon juice if you don't fancy juicing lemons. It's made from real lemons and tastes almost as good as the real thing. A tablespoon of bottled juice is equal to a tablespoon of squeezed lemon – once opened, keep it in the fridge.

# Black Forest Roll

If you have frozen hedgerow fruit, such as blackberries, in the freezer, use them for this impressive dessert.

**Serves 6**

**500 g bag frozen Black Forest fruits**

**2 tablespoons caster sugar, 1 teaspoon reserved**

**2 star anise**

**1 tablespoon cornflour**

**6 x 15 g filo pastry sheets**

**low fat cooking spray**

**2 teaspoons icing sugar, to serve**

**1 teaspoon icing sugar, for dusting**

**2 ProPoints** values per serving
**15 ProPoints** values per recipe

C   **182 calories** per serving

Takes **30 minutes**

V

✳   not recommended

1   Preheat the oven to Gas Mark 6/200°C/fan oven 180°C. Place the fruits, sugar and star anise in a pan. Cover and simmer for 5 minutes until the juices begin to flow. Dissolve the cornflour in 1 tablespoon of cold water and stir into the pan. Increase the heat, bring the fruit to the boil, stirring continuously until thickened. Set aside to cool slightly.

2   Overlap two sheets of filo pastry on a baking tray to form a 30 cm (12 inch) square. Spray with the cooking spray and repeat with another two sheets, spray again and top with a final two sheets. You should have a layered 30 cm square of pastry at the end of this step.

3   Remove the star anise from the cooled fruit mixture and spread the mixture over the filo pastry, leaving a 2 cm (¾ inch) border around the edge. Fold about 1 cm (½ inch) in along the long edges and carefully roll up from the short end. Spray with the cooking spray to seal, sprinkle with the reserved sugar and bake for 10–15 minutes until golden and crisp. Serve warm, with icing sugar dusted on top.

# Banana and Peach Crumble

Banana and peach work beautifully together in this unusual, but delicious crumble.

**Serves 2**

**2 peaches, halved, stoned and sliced into wedges**
**1 banana, sliced**
**50 g (1¾ oz) brown flour**
**25 g (1 oz) low fat spread**
**25 g (1 oz) light brown sugar**

**5 *ProPoints* values per serving**
**10 *ProPoints* values per recipe**

**314 calories** per serving

Takes **10 minutes** to prepare,
**15 minutes** to bake

V

✳ not recommended

1 Preheat the oven to Gas Mark 5/190°C/fan oven 170°C. Place the peach wedges and banana slices in the bottom of a 600 ml (20 fl oz) ovenproof dish. Add 3 tablespoons of water.

2 Place the flour in a bowl and rub in the low fat spread until it resembles breadcrumbs. Stir in the sugar.

3 Spoon the crumble mixture over the fruit and bake for 15 minutes until golden.

**Store cupboard** Brown flour contains more bran than white flour, which gives it a darker colour and stronger flavour. It works well with brown sugar and banana in this tasty crumble.

# Jammy Bread and Butter Pudding

A fun twist on the classic bread and butter pudding, this recipe will be popular with the whole family.

**Serves 6**

**8 medium slices white bread**
**8 heaped teaspoons raspberry jam**
**15 g (½ oz) low fat spread**
**low fat cooking spray**
**100 g (3½ oz) raspberries**
**4 eggs, beaten**
**60 g (2 oz) caster sugar**
**400 ml (14 fl oz) skimmed milk**

1 Preheat the oven to Gas Mark 4/180°C/fan oven 160°C.

2 Make four rounds of jam sandwiches with the bread and jam, then spread the low fat spread over the top of each sandwich.

3 Cut each one into four triangles and place in a baking dish, lightly sprayed with the cooking spray, that holds the sandwiches snugly. Scatter the raspberries in and amongst the sandwiches.

4 Beat the eggs together with the sugar and milk, then pour into the dish, making sure that the bread is evenly covered.

5 Cover with a sheet of foil, lightly sprayed with the cooking spray, then bake for 20 minutes. Remove the foil and bake for a further 10 minutes until golden brown and crisp on top.

7 *ProPoints* values per serving
45 *ProPoints* values per recipe

C **245 calories** per serving

Takes **10 minutes** to prepare,
**30 minutes** to bake

V

✳ not recommended

# Apple and Blackberry Bake

A variation on crumble, using flavoured crispbreads to make a crunchy topping.

**Serves 2**

**200 g (7 oz) eating apples, peeled, cored and chopped**
**140 g (5 oz) blackberries**
**2 teaspoons artificial sweetener**
**2 crispbreads, crumbled**
**½ teaspoon cinnamon**

1  Preheat the oven to Gas Mark 5/190°C/fan oven 170°C. Place the apples and blackberries in a saucepan with 2 tablespoons of water and simmer for 5 minutes until just tender. Sweeten to taste with 1 teaspoon of sweetener and spoon into a shallow ovenproof dish.

2  Mix together the crumbled crispbreads, cinnamon and 1 teaspoon of sweetener. Sprinkle the crumble over the fruit and bake for 10 minutes, until bubbling.

**1 ProPoints** value per serving
**2 ProPoints** values per recipe

C  **98 calories** per serving

Takes **20 minutes**

V

✱  not recommended

# Hot Chocolate Puds

Serve these delicious chocolatey puddings warm from the oven.

**Serves 4**

**low fat cooking spray**
**40 g (1½ oz) low fat spread**
**75 g (2¾ oz) dark chocolate (at least 70% cocoa solids), broken into squares**
**1 egg yolk**
**3 egg whites**
**40 g (1½ oz) caster sugar**
**15 g (½ oz) cocoa powder, sifted plus 1 teaspoon extra, for dusting**

---

© **6 *ProPoints*** values per serving
**25 *ProPoints*** values per recipe

C **272 calories** per serving

🕑 Takes **30 minutes**

V

✱ not recommended

1 Lightly spray the base of four 150 ml (5 fl oz) pudding basins or ramekins with the cooking spray and line with baking parchment. Preheat the oven to Gas Mark 6/200°C/fan oven 180°C.

2 Simmer some water in a pan and then, in a heatproof bowl over the top of the pan, melt the low fat spread and chocolate together. Stir until smooth, remove from the heat and leave to cool slightly. Beat in the egg yolk.

3 In a clean, grease-free bowl, whisk the egg whites until they form stiff peaks. Whisk in the caster sugar a spoonful at a time.

4 Add a spoonful of egg white to the chocolate mixture and stir quickly, with a metal spoon, to combine. Add half of the remaining egg white and fold in carefully. Add the sifted cocoa and remaining egg white, working carefully but swiftly until the mixture is fully blended.

5 Spoon the mixture into the pudding basins or ramekins and bake for 8–10 minutes, until the top is raised and firm to the touch. Leave in the dishes for 2–3 minutes and then carefully turn out on to serving plates. Dust with the cocoa before serving immediately.

**Cooking basics** To melt chocolate: place a saucepan of water on the hob and bring to the boil. Reduce the heat until it is gently simmering. Break the chocolate into chunks and place it in a heatproof bowl. Put the bowl over the saucepan of water so that the base does not touch the water. Let the chocolate melt gently.

# Summer Fruit Gâteau

When there are lots of succulent summer fruits available, make the most of them with this mouth-watering gâteau.

**Makes 8 slices**

**For the sponge**
**3 eggs**
**175 g (6 oz) caster sugar**
**175 g (6 oz) plain white flour**
**finely grated zest of an orange**
**2 tablespoons orange juice**

**For the filling**
**150 ml (5 fl oz) low fat strawberry**
   **fromage frais**
**125 g (4½ oz) fresh strawberries, hulled**
**100 g (3½ oz) fresh raspberries**
**1 nectarine, stoned and diced**
**50 g (1¾ oz) fresh blueberries**
**1 teaspoon icing sugar, to dust**

℃ **6 *ProPoints*** values per serving
**46 *ProPoints*** values per recipe

C **230 calories** per serving.

☺ Takes **25 minutes** to prepare +
**1 hour** cooling, **15 minutes** to bake

V

✱ recommended (see Tip)

1 Preheat the oven to Gas Mark 5/190°C/fan oven 170°C. Line the base of two 18 cm (7 inch) round cake tins with non stick baking parchment.

2 Using electric beaters, whisk the eggs and caster sugar together for at least 5 minutes until very pale and fluffy. Sift the flour into the mixture and fold it in carefully, using a metal spoon – don't stir it too much or you will knock the air out of the mixture.

3 Carefully fold in the orange zest and orange juice, and then divide the mixture between the two prepared tins. Bake for 12–15 minutes until the sponges are golden and springy to the touch. Transfer them to a wire rack and allow them to cool completely.

4 When cool, spread one of the cakes with the fromage frais, scatter over most of the prepared fruits, reserving a few for the top, and then place the other sponge cake on top. Dust the surface with sifted icing sugar and top with the reserved fruit.

**Tip** You can freeze the sponges. Wrap them individually and freeze for up to 2 months. Allow them to defrost at room temperature and then assemble the gâteau with the filling ingredients.

# Orange Semolina Puddings

Semolina pudding was never this yummy at school.

**Serves 4**

**25 g (1 oz) semolina**
**450 ml (16 fl oz) skimmed milk**
**artificial sweetener, to taste**
**finely grated zest and segments of a large**
**  orange**
**2 large eggs, separated**
**1 tablespoon caster sugar**

---

**3 ProPoints** values per serving
**13 ProPoints** values per recipe

**135 calories** per serving

Takes **20 minutes**

V

* not recommended

1 Preheat the oven to Gas Mark 5/190°C/fan oven 170°C.

2 Put the semolina in a saucepan and stir in the milk. Bring to the boil, stirring constantly until thickened. Reduce the heat and cook gently for 2–3 minutes.

3 Remove from the heat, leave to cool for a few minutes then add sweetener to taste. Stir in the orange zest and egg yolks. Divide the mixture between four individual heatproof dishes or ramekins. Top with the orange segments.

4 Beat the egg whites in a grease-free bowl until they hold their shape. Whisk in the sugar then pile this on top of the desserts. Bake for 3–5 minutes until golden brown. Serve at once.

# Peach Angel Roulade

It is worth taking a bit of time to assemble this impressive roulade, served with peaches and yogurt.

**Serves 6**

low fat cooking spray
5 egg whites
50 g (1¾ oz) plain flour
a pinch of salt
110 g (4 oz) caster sugar
410 g can peach slices in natural juice, drained and chopped
zest of ½ a lime
150 g pot 0% fat Greek yogurt

3 *ProPoints* values per serving
20 *ProPoints* values per recipe

C   **144 calories** per serving

⊘   Takes **25 minutes** + cooling

V

✱   not recommended

1 Preheat the oven to Gas Mark 4/180°C/fan oven 160°C. Line a 20 x 30 cm (8 x 12 inch) Swiss roll tin with baking parchment and lightly mist with the cooking spray.

2 Whisk the egg whites to stiff peaks in a large bowl. Sift in the flour, a pinch of salt and all but 2 teaspoons of the sugar and fold together. Spread out in the tin and bake on the centre shelf of the oven for 12–15 minutes until set, golden and beginning to pull away from the edges of the tin.

3 Lay another sheet of baking parchment on the work surface and sprinkle with the reserved sugar. Turn out the angel sponge cake on to the paper. Peel off the lining paper and roll up the roulade from one long side, wrapping the sugared paper inside as you go.

4 Leave to cool. Mix the peaches with the lime zest and set aside.

5 To serve, unroll the roulade, spread with the yogurt then scatter the peaches over. Roll up and cut into slices.

# Creamy Orange Puddings

These individual sponge puddings are deliciously smooth and tangy.

**Serves 6**

**4 oranges**
**low fat cooking spray**
**300 g (10½ oz) extra light low fat**
**soft cheese**
**2 large eggs, separated, plus 1 egg white**
**75 g (2¾ oz) icing sugar, sieved**
**1 tablespoon cornflour**

**4 ProPoints** values per serving
**25 ProPoints** values per recipe

**190 calories** per serving

Takes **15 minutes** to prepare + cooling,
**20 minutes** to bake

V

✻  not recommended

1  Preheat the oven to Gas Mark 7/220°C/fan oven 200°C.

2  Finely grate the zest from two of the oranges and set aside. Peel the oranges and use a serrated knife to remove all the bitter white pith, keeping the segments intact. Cut horizontally into 8 mm (¼ inch) slices.

3  Lightly spray the insides of six 125 ml (4 fl oz) basins or small ramekin dishes with the cooking spray. In a large bowl, beat together the soft cheese, egg yolks, half the icing sugar, cornflour and the orange zest.

4  Whisk the egg whites in a grease-free bowl until stiff, then whisk in the remaining icing sugar. Beat a tablespoon of the meringue mixture into the soft cheese mixture then gently fold in the rest.

5  Arrange the orange slices over the base and sides of each basin then fill with the cheese mixture. Arrange the basins in a roasting dish filled with 2.5 cm (1 inch) of water and cover lightly with greaseproof paper. Bake in the preheated oven for 15–20 minutes, or until the filling is still slightly wobbly.

6  Leave to cool for 5 minutes before turning out on to individual serving plates. Serve immediately.

# Magic Mocha Pudding

A delightful pudding that has a light sponge on top, concealing a delicious hot mocha sauce inside.

**Serves 6**

**125 g (4½ oz) self raising flour**
**40 g (1½ oz) cocoa powder**
**50 g (1¾ oz) caster sugar**
**1 teaspoon vanilla essence**
**125 ml (4 fl oz) semi skimmed milk**

For the mocha sauce

**50 g (1¾ oz) demerara sugar**
**1 teaspoon instant coffee powder**
**350 ml (12 fl oz) boiling water**

---

**5 *ProPoints*** values per serving
**27 *ProPoints*** values per recipe

C   **165 calories** per serving

Takes **10 minutes** to prepare,
**45 minutes** to bake

V

✳   not recommended

1 Preheat the oven to Gas Mark 4/180°C/fan oven 160°C.

2 Sieve the flour and 2 level tablespoons of the cocoa powder into a bowl. Stir in the caster sugar, vanilla essence and milk, beating the mixture until smooth. Spread the mixture into a 1.2 litre (2 pint) baking or soufflé dish.

3 Mix the demerara sugar with the remaining cocoa powder and sprinkle it evenly over the creamed mixture. Dissolve the coffee in the boiling water and then pour it all over the pudding.

4 Bake for 45 minutes until risen and the sponge mixture is firm to the touch. Serve immediately.

# Tropical Fruit Crumble

Just a tiny amount of rum gives this crumble a tropical flavour.

**Serves 4**

low fat cooking spray

2 bananas, sliced thinly

225 g (8 oz) canned pineapple rings in fruit juice, cut into pieces, juice reserved

30 ml (1 fl oz) white, dark or spiced rum

140 g packet crumble mix

50 g (1¾ oz) unsweetened wholewheat muesli with dried fruit

---

6 *ProPoints* values per serving
26 *ProPoints* values per recipe

C   306 calories per serving

Takes **10 minutes** to prepare,
**35 minutes** to bake

V

✱   not recommended

1 Preheat the oven to Gas Mark 5/190°C/fan oven 170°C. Lightly spray a deep, 15 cm (6 inch) round, ovenproof dish with the cooking spray.

2 Layer the bananas and the pineapple with the juice and rum in the dish.

3 Mix the crumble with the muesli and spread this mixture over the fruit.

4 Bake for 30–35 minutes until golden brown. Serve hot or cold.

# Lemon Meringue Pots

**3** ProPoints value

These individual lemon meringue desserts are a fantastic way to end a perfect meal.

**Serves 4**

**4 eggs, separated**
**300 ml (10 fl oz) skimmed milk**
**finely grated zest of 2 lemons, and the juice**
**of a lemon**
**25 g (1 oz) low fat spread**
**6 teaspoons artificial sweetener**

---

**3** *ProPoints* values per serving
**13** *ProPoints* values per recipe

**166 calories** per serving

Takes **30 minutes**, **15 minutes** to prepare,
**15 minutes** to bake

**V**

* not recommended

1 Preheat the oven to Gas Mark 4/180°C/fan oven 160°C. Beat the egg yolks.

2 Bring the milk to the boil, remove from the heat and add the egg yolks. Return to the heat and cook, stirring continuously until thickened.

3 Stir in the lemon zest, juice and low fat spread. Add 1 teaspoon of sweetener. Spoon into four 150 ml (5 fl oz) ovenproof ramekins and set aside.

4 In a clean bowl, whisk the egg whites until stiff peaks appear. Sprinkle over 5 teaspoons of sweetener and whisk to combine. Spoon the meringue on top of the lemon custard, spreading it to the edges to seal. Bake for 12–15 minutes until golden. Serve immediately.

**Eat wisely** These meringue pots are ideal for portion control as they are made in individual pots.

# Summer Fruit Profiteroles

The creamy filling for these squidgy profiteroles is Quark, a low fat curd cheese with a smooth texture.

**Serves 6 (makes 18 profiteroles)**

**For the profiteroles**
**75 g (2¾ oz) plain flour**
**a pinch of salt**
**60 g (2 oz) low fat spread**
**2 eggs, beaten**

**For the sauce**
**250 g (9 oz) frozen summer fruits, defrosted**
**1½ tablespoons artificial sweetener**

**For the filling**
**250 g (9 oz) Quark**
**1 teaspoon vanilla extract**
**2 tablespoons artificial sweetener**

4 *ProPoints* values per serving
22 *ProPoints* values per recipe

C  197 calories per serving

Takes **20 minutes** to prepare + cooling,
**25 minutes** to bake

✳  not recommended

1 Preheat the oven to Gas Mark 6/200°C/fan oven 180°C.

2 Sift the flour and a pinch of salt on to a piece of greaseproof paper that has been folded in half and then opened out again.

3 Place the low fat spread in a non stick saucepan with 150 ml (5 fl oz) of cold water and bring to the boil. Remove from the heat and tip in the flour, stirring with a wooden spoon until the mixture comes together in a smooth ball. Sit the pan in a basin of cold water until the dough is cool.

4 Gradually beat in the eggs, until you have a smooth batter that drops easily from the spoon. Scatter droplets of water over two baking trays, then place nine heaped teaspoonfuls of the batter on to each tray, leaving room for the profiteroles to rise.

5 Bake for 18–20 minutes until the profiteroles are well risen and quite brown. Make a small hole in each one to release the steam then return to the oven for a further 5 minutes to crisp up. Cool on a wire rack.

6 Blend the berries to a purée in a food processor or liquidiser, then pass through a sieve to remove any pips and seeds. Stir in the sweetener.

7 Mix the Quark, vanilla extract and sweetener together. Split the profiteroles open and stuff each one with a teaspoon of filling. Serve three profiteroles per person, with the sauce poured over the top.

**Tips** Don't fill the profiteroles too far in advance (30 minutes at most) as they will start to go soft. Quark curd cheese can be used in both sweet and savoury recipes. It is available from the dairy chiller cabinet in most supermarkets.

# White Chocolate Soufflé

The temperamental soufflé is easy in a modern oven – amaze your guests with this splendid pudding.

**Serves 4**

**low fat cooking spray**
**3 teaspoons icing sugar**
**25 g (1 oz) cornflour**
**250 ml (9 fl oz) skimmed milk**
**100 g (3½ oz) white chocolate, broken into pieces**
**1 teaspoon vanilla extract**
**25 g (1 oz) caster sugar**
**2 egg yolks**
**5 egg whites**

1 Prepare a 1 litre (1¾ pint) soufflé dish by spraying it with the cooking spray and then dusting it with the icing sugar. Preheat the oven to Gas Mark 7/220°C/fan oven 200°C.

2 In a small bowl, mix the cornflour to a smooth paste with a few tablespoons of the milk. Put the remainder of the milk in a saucepan with the chocolate, vanilla and sugar. Stir over a gentle heat until the chocolate and sugar have melted and dissolved.

3 Pour in the cornflour paste, stirring constantly, and then bring the mixture to the boil. Boil for 1 minute, stirring vigorously all the time. Allow to cool a little and then beat in the egg yolks.

4 Meanwhile, in a clean, grease-free bowl, whisk the egg whites until very fluffy then gently fold them into the chocolate mixture. Fill the soufflé dish and bake for 40 minutes without opening the oven door. Serve immediately with a dusting of icing sugar.

**7 *ProPoints*** values per serving
**30 *ProPoints*** values per recipe

C **270 calories** per serving

Takes **20 minutes** to prepare + cooling, **40 minutes** to bake

V

✱ not recommended

**Tip** The soufflé can be prepared ahead of time up to step 3.

# Lemon Curd Sponges

These light sponge puddings have a luscious and delightfully tart lemon curd sauce poured over them.

**Serves 4**

**low fat cooking spray**
**60 g (2 oz) low fat spread**
**60 g (2 oz) caster sugar**
**1 egg**

**100 g (3½ oz) self raising flour**
**grated zest of a small lemon plus**
**  2 tablespoons juice**
**4 heaped teaspoons lemon curd**

1 Preheat the oven to Gas Mark 4/180°C/fan oven 160°C. Lightly spray four mini pudding basins with the cooking spray and place them on a baking tray.

2 Using an electric whisk, beat together the low fat spread, sugar, egg, flour, lemon zest and 1 tablespoon of lemon juice for 2 minutes. Spoon into the pudding basins to come about halfway up, then bake on the centre shelf for 15 minutes.

3 Meanwhile, in a small saucepan, stir together the lemon curd, 1 tablespoon of lemon juice and 1 tablespoon of water. Heat gently to make the sauce.

4 Turn the puddings out of the moulds and serve warm with the sauce spooned over.

**7 ProPoints** values per serving
**29 ProPoints** values per recipe

C **240 calories** per serving

Takes **25 minutes**

V

\* recommended (without the sauce)

# Hazelnut Meringue Roulade

This light meringue roulade, with hazelnut and coffee flavours, is the perfect end to a meal.

Serves 8

**5 egg whites**
**200 g (7 oz) caster sugar**
**50 g (1¾ oz) hazelnuts, chopped finely and**
**    toasted, 1 tablespoon reserved**
**2 x 250 g tubs Quark**
**2 teaspoons instant coffee, dissolved in**
**    1 tablespoon hot water**

5 *ProPoints* values per serving
42 *ProPoints* values per recipe

C  **191 calories** per serving

Takes **25 minutes** to prepare + cooling,
**1 hour** to bake

V

✳  not recommended

1  Preheat the oven to Gas Mark 2/150°C/fan oven 130°C. Line a 33 x 23 cm (13 inch x 9 inch) Swiss roll tin with non stick baking parchment.

2  In a clean, grease-free bowl, whisk the egg whites until they form stiff peaks. Adding 1 tablespoon at a time, gradually whisk 150 g (5½ oz) sugar into the egg whites, making sure it is completely combined before adding the next tablespoon. The egg white mixture should be stiff and glossy. Now carefully fold in the hazelnuts.

3  Spread the mixture evenly over the tin and bake for 1 hour until golden and crisp on the outside. Cool in the tin before turning out on to a sheet of greaseproof paper and removing the baking parchment.

4  Mix together the remaining sugar, Quark and coffee. Spread this over the meringue, leaving an edge of about 2 cm (¾ inch) at the short end farthest away from you. Carefully roll up (it will crack but don't worry) and place on a serving plate with the seam side down. Serve decorated with the reserved hazelnuts.

# Citrus Chocolate Spice Pudding

If you've never cooked a sponge like this, you're in for a treat, as it literally rises in front of your eyes.

**Serves 4**

**low fat cooking spray**
**100 g (3½ oz) grapefruit segments**
**½ teaspoon ground ginger (optional)**
**4 heaped teaspoons low calorie marmalade**
**50 g (1¾ oz) caster sugar**
**2 eggs**
**50 g (1¾ oz) self raising flour**
**15 g (½ oz) cocoa powder**

**5 ProPoints** values per serving
**18 ProPoints** values per recipe

**175 calories** per serving

Takes **20 minutes**

V

\* not recommended

1 Spray a 1.2 litre (2 pint) pudding basin with the cooking spray.

2 Put the grapefruit segments into the basin. Mix the ginger, if using, and 2 teaspoons of water into the marmalade, then spoon this mixture over the grapefruit.

3 Using an electric beater, whisk the sugar and eggs together until very light and thick; this will take about 5 minutes.

4 Sift the flour and cocoa powder together, then gently fold into the whisked mixture, using a large metal spoon to retain as much air as possible. Transfer this mixture to the pudding basin.

5 To cook in the microwave, cover the basin with microwave safe cling film and pierce it 2 or 3 times. Cook in the microwave on High for 2½–3 minutes, or until risen and spongy. Allow to stand for 3 minutes before serving.

**Tip** To cook in a steamer, cover the pudding with foil or greaseproof paper and steam for 1 hour 10 minutes, making sure that the steamer does not boil dry.

**Variation** Use a peeled and segmented orange – with all the pith removed – instead of the grapefruit segments. The **ProPoints** values will remain the same.

# Pear and Ginger Tarte Tatin

3 ProPoints value

Pear and ginger go beautifully together in this easy dessert.

**Serves 6**

**2 pieces stem ginger in syrup, chopped finely, plus 2 tablespoons syrup from the jar**

**2 x 210 g cans pear halves in natural juice, drained**

**1 teaspoon plain flour**

**125 g (4½ oz) puff pastry**

---

3 *ProPoints* values per serving
19 *ProPoints* values per recipe

**C**   **126 calories** per serving

Takes **10 minutes** to prepare,
**20 minutes** to bake

**V**

**\*** not recommended

1 Preheat the oven to Gas Mark 6/200°C/fan oven 180°C.

2 Place the chopped stem ginger and syrup in the base of a tarte tatin dish or a 24 cm (9½ inch) round cake tin, then arrange the pear halves to fit in snugly, rounded side down.

3 Dust the work surface with the flour and roll out the pastry to fit neatly inside the dish or tin. Place on top of the pear halves and then tuck the pastry around the fruit at the edges.

4 Place on a baking tray and bake for 20 minutes or until the pastry is well risen and crisp. Turn out on to a plate to serve.

# Key Lime Pie

A slice of pie is a favourite American dessert. This one originates from the Florida Keys, where limes are grown.

**Serves 10**

60 g (2 oz) low fat spread
140 g (5 oz) reduced fat digestive biscuits, crushed
3 eggs, separated
405 g can skimmed condensed milk
finely grated zest and juice of 3 limes
3–4 drops green food colouring
25 g (1 oz) caster sugar

**6 ProPoints** values per serving
**62 ProPoints** values per recipe

**C**   **235 calories** per serving

Takes **15 minutes** to prepare + **15 minutes** chilling + cooling, **25 minutes** to bake

**V**

✳   not recommended

1 Melt the low fat spread in a medium saucepan and add the biscuit crumbs, stirring to coat them all. Tip the coated crumbs into a 23 cm (9 inch) pie or flan dish, pressing them over the base. Chill in the fridge for about 15 minutes.

2 Preheat the oven to Gas Mark 4/180°C/fan oven 160°C.

3 Beat the egg yolks and condensed milk together, and then stir in the lime zest and juice. Add a few drops of food colouring to make the mixture pale green. Pour the mixture over the prepared biscuit crumb base and bake for 15–20 minutes, until set.

4 Meanwhile, in a grease-free bowl and using an electric beater, whisk the egg whites until they hold their shape. Add the sugar gradually, whisking well to make stiff, glossy peaks.

5 Pile the meringue mixture on top of the lime pie, spreading it over the surface. Return it to the oven and bake for about 5–6 minutes, until the topping is golden brown.

6 Let the pie cool for about 15 minutes before serving, or you can serve it chilled.

**Tip** Egg whites will not whisk successfully if there is the slightest trace of grease, including egg yolk, in the bowl or on the beaters, so make sure everything has just been washed in hot, soapy water before you begin.

# Blueberry Baked Cheesecake

Baked cheesecakes tend to crack if they cool too quickly; to avoid this, leave the cooked cheesecake in the turned off oven to cool.

**Serves 10**

**6 large caramel rice cakes**
**2 ripe bananas, mashed**
**500 g (1 lb 2 oz) Quark**
**200 g (7 oz) very low fat plain fromage frais**
**3 eggs**
**2 teaspoons vanilla extract**
**3 tablespoons artificial sweetener**
**150 g (5½ oz) fresh blueberries**

---

**2 ProPoints** values per serving
**23 ProPoints** values per recipe

C **181 calories** per serving

Takes **15 minutes** to prepare + cooling + chilling, **35 minutes** to bake

V

* not recommended

1 Preheat the oven to Gas Mark 4/180°C/fan oven 160°C.

2 Process the rice cakes to rough crumbs in a food processor, then mix into the mashed bananas.

3 Press into the base of a 20 cm (8 inch) springform cake tin, then bake in the oven for 10 minutes until firm.

4 Remove from the oven and reduce the temperature to Gas Mark 2/150°C/fan oven 130°C.

5 Wipe out the processor bowl then whizz together the Quark, fromage frais, eggs, vanilla and sweetener until smooth.

6 Pour half of the mixture over the cheesecake base and scatter with half the blueberries. Add the remaining cheesecake mixture and blueberries and shake gently to level the surface.

7 Bake in the oven for 35 minutes, until the cheesecake is set in the centre but still slightly wobbly. Turn off the oven, but leave the cheesecake in the oven as it cools.

8 Chill before serving, then carefully unmould and cut into slices.

# Index

### A

Apple
  American apple pie 98
  Apple and apricot muffins 68
  Apple and blackberry bake 131
  Apple and rosemary cake 24
  Apple and walnut pie 95
  Apple strudel 122
  French apple tarts 114
  Raspberry and apple cake 26
  Strawberry and apple filo tart 108
Apricot
  Apple and apricot muffins 68
  Vanilla and apricot loaf 30

### B

Baked lemon pudding 126
Banana
  Baked banana with passion fruit 123
  Banana and fig loaf 79
  Banana and peach crumble 128
  Banana and sultana loaf 25
  Banana muffins 66
  Banana oat bars 50
Better brownies 34
Biscuits
  Banana oat bars 50
  Blueberry cookies 52
  Cinnamon cookies 76
  Cookies 74
  Oat and cherry biscuits 75
  Strawberry shortcakes 59

Blackberry
  Apple and blackberry bake 131
  Fresh blackberry muffins 70
Black Forest roll 127
Blueberry
  Blueberry baked cheesecake 156
  Blueberry cookies 52
Bread and butter pudding, jammy 130
Bread and rolls
  Easy rosemary beer bread 89
  Healthy herb bread 84
  Mediterranean bread 86
  Olive and tomato rolls with basil 58
  Orchard fruit and ginger tea bread 19
  Potato and spring onion bread 85
  Quick and easy wholemeal bread 88
Buns
  Golden raspberry buns 82
  Italian buns 78
  Cinnamon prune buns 80

### C

Cakes
  Apple and rosemary cake 24
  Banana and sultana loaf 25
  Better brownies 34
  Carrot and pineapple squares 46
  Carrot and sultana cake 33
  Chocolate mocha fudge cake 16
  Courgette tea cake 32
  Creamy orange gâteau 40
  Golden pumpkin tray bake 29

Hazelnut cake 38
  Lemon and ginger roulade 36
  Lemon drizzle cake 15
  Lemon madeleines 42
  Low fat sticky gingerbread 28
  Moist mango cake 14
  Orchard fruit and ginger tea bread 19
  Peach crumble cake 12
  Pear and chocolate cake 10
  Petal cakes 39
  Raspberry and apple cake 26
  Snow covered Christmas cake 43
  Squash, ginger cake 22
  Stem ginger cake 18
  Triple decker lime cream sponge 44
  White chocolate and raspberry cake 20
Carrot
  Carrot and pineapple squares 46
  Carrot and sultana cake 33
Cheese and tomato muffins 60
Cheesecake, blueberry baked 156
Cheesecake, lime, tarts 106
Cheesecake, tiny, tarts 104
Cherry, oat and, biscuits 75
Chocolate
  Chocolate mocha fudge cake 16
  Chocolate roulade with raspberry crush 120
  Citrus chocolate sponge pudding 150
  Hot chocolate puds 132
  Pear and chocolate cake 10
  White chocolate and raspberry cake 20
  White chocolate soufflé 146

Christmas cake, snow covered 43

Cinnamon

    Cinnamon cookies 76

    Cinnamon prune buns 80

Citrus chocolate sponge pudding 150

Cookies 74

Courgette tea cake 32

Cranberry muffins 64

Creamy orange gâteau 40

Creamy orange puddings 138

Crumble

    Banana and peach crumble 128

    Tropical fruit crumble 14

D

Deluxe mince parcels 111

E

Easy rosemary beer bread 89

Eccles swirls 94

F

Fig

    Banana and fig loaf 79

    Fresh fig tart 102

Filo pastry

    Apple and walnut pie 95

    Deluxe mince parcels 111

    Eccles swirls 94

    Fruity filo tarts 99

    Lime cheesecake tarts 106

    Strawberry and apple filo tart 108

Flapjacks, raisin and honey 71

French apple tarts 114

Fresh blackberry muffins 70

Fresh fig tart 102

Fruit scones 56

Fruity filo tarts 99

G

Gâteau

    Creamy orange gâteau 40

    Lemon, almond and strawberry gâteau 124

    Summer fruit gâteau 134

Ginger

    Lemon and ginger roulade 36

    Low fat sticky gingerbread 28

    Orchard fruit and ginger tea bread 19

    Pear and ginger tarte tatin 152

    Squash, ginger cake 22

    Stem ginger cake 18

Going for Gold 72

Golden raspberry buns 82

Golden pumpkin tray bake 29

H

Hazelnut

    Hazelnut cake 38

    Hazelnut meringue roulade 148

Healthy herb bread 84

Hot chocolate puds 132

I

Italian buns 78

J

Jammy bread and butter pudding 130

K

Key lime pie 154

L

Lemon

    Baked lemon pudding 126

    Lemon, almond and strawberry gâteau 124

    Lemon and ginger roulade 36

    Lemon curd sponges 147

    Lemon drizzle cake 15

    Lemon madeleines 42

    Lemon meringue pots 142

Lime

    Lime Cheesecake tarts 106

    Key lime pie 154

    Triple decker lime cream sponge 44

Low fat sticky gingerbread 28

M

Madeleines, lemon 42

Magic mocha pudding 140

Mango, moist, cake 14

Marmalade muffins 62

Mediterranean bread 86

Meringue

    Hazelnut meringue roulade 148

    Key lime pie 154

    Lemon meringue pots 142

Mocha

    Chocolate mocha fudge cake 16

    Magic mocha pudding 140

Moist mango cake 14

Muffins

    Apple and apricot muffins 68

    Banana muffins 66

    Cheese and tomato muffins 60

    Cranberry muffins 64

    Fresh blackberry muffins 70

    Marmalade muffins 62

    Must have muffins 65

N

Nectarine and strawberry tart 92

Nutmeg and yogurt scone squares 54

O

Oats

    Banana oat bars 50

Oat and cherry biscuits 75
Raisin and honey flapjacks 71
Olive and tomato rolls with basil 58
Orange
Creamy orange gâteau 40
Creamy orange puddings 138
Orange semolina pudding 136
Orchard fruit and ginger tea bread 19

P
Peach
Peach angel roulade 137
Banana and peach crumble 128
Peach crumble cake 12
Pear
Pear and almond tart 116
Pear and chocolate cake 10
Pear and ginger tarte tatin 152
Pecan treacle tart 112
Petal cakes 39
Pies
American apple pie 98
Apple and walnut pie 95
Key lime pie 154
Plum pie 110
Pineapple
Carrot and pineapple squares 46
Pineapple tarte tatin 100
Plum pie 110
Potato and spring onion bread 85
Profiteroles, summer fruit 144
Prune
Cinnamon prune buns 80
Puddings
Baked lemon pudding 126
Citrus chocolate sponge pudding 150
Creamy orange puddings 138
Hot chocolate puds 132

Jammy bread and butter pudding 130
Magic mocha pudding 140
Orange semolina pudding 136
Pumpkin
Golden pumpkin tray bake 29

Q
Quick and easy wholemeal bread 88

R
Raisin and honey flapjacks, 71
Raspberry
Chocolate roulade with raspberry crush 120
Fruity filo tarts 99
Golden raspberry buns 82
Raspberry and apple cake 26
White chocolate and raspberry cake 20
Rhubarb lasagne 105
Roulade
Chocolate roulade with raspberry crush 120
Hazelnut meringue roulade 148
Lemon and ginger roulade 36
Peach angel roulade 137

S
Saffron scones 55
Scones
Fruit scones 56
Going for gold 72
Nutmeg and yogurt scone squares 54
Saffron scones 55
Semolina, orange, pudding 136
Snow covered Christmas cake 43
Soufflé, white chocolate 146
Squishy squash ginger cake 22
Stem ginger cake 18
Strawberry
Lemon, almond and strawberry gâteau 124
Nectarine and strawberry tart 92

Strawberry and apple filo tart 108
Strawberry shortcakes 59
Summer fruit gâteau 134
Summer fruit profiteroles 144
Sultanas
Banana and sultana loaf 25
Carrot and sultana cake 33

T
Tarte tatin, pear and ginger 152
Tarte tatin, pineapple 100
Tarts
French apple tarts 114
Fresh fig tart 102
Fruity filo tarts 99
Lime cheesecake tarts 106
Nectarine and strawberry tart 92
Pear and almond tart 116
Pecan treacle tart 112
Pineapple tarte tatin 100
Strawberry and apple filo tart 108
Tiny cheesecake tarts 104
Yorkshire curd tarts 96
Tiny cheesecake tarts 104
Triple decker lime cream sponge 44
Tropical fruit crumble 141

V
Vanilla and apricot loaf 30

W
Walnut, apple and, pie 95
White chocolate and raspberry cake 20
White chocolate soufflé 146

Y
Yorkshire curd tarts 96